To Dick with many
thanks

GREAT BOOKS
AND
SMALL GROUPS

Great Books
and
Small Groups

By JAMES A. DAVIS

with the assistance of
RUTH URSULA GEBHARD
HERBERT HAMILTON
CAROLYN HUSON
JOE L. SPAETH

The Free Press of Glencoe, Inc.

A DIVISION OF THE CROWELL-COLLIER PUBLISHING COMPANY

Foreword

The Fund for Adult Education is delighted to welcome this latest addition to the growing literature of research in the important field of adult liberal education.

In 1957, The Fund for Adult Education, an independent agency established by The Ford Foundation, commissioned the National Opinion Research Center to make a study of the participants in The Great Books program and of some of the effects upon them of their participation. A first report was submitted to the Fund in 1958 and copies were sent to a number of educational and research institutions and libraries. Slightly abridged, it has now been published under the title *A Study of Participants in The Great Books Program* —one in a series of "Studies in Adult Group Learning in the Liberal Arts."

The present report, made under a continuation of the original grant, is a more detailed study of factors which tend to retain members within on-going liberal education programs. While the methods and principles applied here by Dr. Davis and his associates are undoubtedly familiar to students of social research, their application to study-discussion programs and processes is an original and important contribution. We believe it should prove of great practical usefulness in the hands of educational program administrators, and we hope that it will spark further studies of key factors in group participation.

C. SCOTT FLETCHER
President, The Fund for Adult Education

Preface

This is the third and last in a series of reports by National Opinion Research Center on a national survey of participants in The Great Books program. This report may be read independently, but its aims will perhaps become clearer if we review the history of the project.

In 1957 The Fund for Adult Education commissioned NORC to conduct a study of the effects of Great Books on members of the discussion groups. During December, 1957, NORC interviewers attended the meetings of 172 groups, sampled on a national basis. The sample is described in Chapter One, which also presents a brief discussion of Great Books. A completed report [1] was submitted to the sponsors in September, 1958. The report was long and detailed and we shall not attempt to summarize it here. Basically, it covered a description of the members, some guesses about the audience from which the members are recruited, and a detailed statistical examination of data on the effects of participation.

We wished to determine whether exposure to the program leads to changes in members' knowledge, reading habits,

1. James A. Davis, Lathrop Vickery Beale, and Ruth Ursula Gebhard, *The Great Books Program: A National Survey* (Chicago: National Opinion Research Center, 1958).

attitudes, and civic participation. In theory, a controlled experiment is the only airtight way of answering these questions, but this was impossible, and we were forced to rely upon statistical comparisons between beginning and advanced members. Now, if there are effects, they will show up in such comparisons, but it does not follow that if differences turn up that they must be due to the program. We were particularly concerned about the possibility that dropouts could lead to spurious findings. For example, we found that advanced year members had much higher knowledge of liberal arts than did beginners. This suggested that exposure to Great Books leads to increased information about liberal arts. However, if members with low knowledge tend disproportionately to drop out of the program, we would get a spurious difference between beginning and advanced members even if the program did not have any effect on knowledge.

While we did the best we could with the statistical tricks available, at the time of the completion of our report we were still worried about the drop-out problem. Therefore, we proposed to The Fund for Adult Education that we collect follow-up data in order to locate actual drop-outs and then re-examine our original findings with these new data as controls. The Fund accepted our proposal, and during the Fall of 1958 we collected our follow-up information. We did not get our information from the group members, rather, from questionnaires to leaders and informal questions to community coordinators we managed to determine the continuation status of 92 per cent of the people in our original sample.

Subsequently, we re-analysed parts of our original data, and managed to get a much more adequate (although far from perfect) picture of the program's effects by using the actual drop-out data as a statistical control. A second report, embodying this re-analysis, and summarizing the highlights of the first report was delivered to The Fund for Adult Education in the winter of 1959.

This report has subsequently been published.[2] Under our continuation grant we were able to use the drop-out data, originally collected as a statistical control, to examine the substantive problem of program retention in Great Books.

Essentially this report consists of a series of studies, all oriented around the problem of locating and understanding the factors which keep people in Great Books and those which lead them to drop out of the program.

Now, our data can be looked at as either 1,909 individuals who happen to be sampled in 172 discussion groups, or as 172 discussion groups which happen to contain 1,909 individuals. This form of sample, by accident, enabled us to make a much more sophisticated attack on the problem than we might have otherwise. In particular, it led us to wonder how much of the retention process could be allocated to individual factors (the characteristics of people as individuals which affect their continuation) and how much to group factors (the characteristics of groups as groups which affect the retention of their members). This duality is the heart of this study, which consists, in essence, of an attempt to view the same set of variables simultaneously as individual variables and as group variables.

While the difference between group and individual factors is axiomatic among sociologists, such analyses present tricky technical problems when we try to make statistical analyses of actual data. Chapter One of this book is devoted to discussion of the research questions and an exposition of the techniques we developed to answer them. While the chapter is devoid of substantive findings, the rest of the study flows from the ideas developed there, and the reader is warned

2. James A. Davis, Lathrop Vickery Beale, and Ruth Ursula Gebbard, *A Study of Participants in The Great Books Program*, "Studies in Adult Group Learning, Number Three" (White Plains, New York: The Fund for Adult Education, 1960).

that Chapter One is a prerequisite for the rest of the book.

Chapter Two describes the sample, the program, and some of the salient characteristics of the participants. In particular, it stresses their locations in and the roles they play in the larger social structure because of the importance of these variables for understanding program retention.

Chapter Three describes the role systems within the small discussion groups. It attempts to assess the degree to which there are institutionalized roles in these small groups and the factors related to differences among the members in the kind of role they play and whether they play any role at all.

Chapters Four, Five, and Six are the detailed analyses of the factors related to drop-out from the program. Actually, they constitute a single analysis, but for purposes of digestibility, they have been divided into three parts. Chapter Four treats formal and informal role systems in the groups and certain variables closely related to them. Chapter Five treats family and community roles outside the groups. Chapter Six treats intellectual abilities, religious factors, and political party preference. As the chapters develop, a system of interlocking variables which are important for group membership retention is described and speculations are advanced as to its workings.

Chapter Seven reviews the major findings, states the general conclusions of the study, and offers some few practical suggestions for the operation of the program.

It is perhaps appropriate that a study of small groups be conducted not by an individual, but by a small group. A complete listing of the people involved in this research would probably involve close to 100 names, but I should like to convey special thanks to the following.

This study was commissioned by The Fund for Adult Education, and I should like to thank them, and particularly Mr. G. H. Griffiths, vice-president of the Fund, not only for their obvious generosity in providing the funds, but also for encouraging us to follow what paths we chose in our research, rather than to hike down a predetermined route. Money is not hard to come by in social research, but freedom is.

Mr. Orace Johnson, Miss Lilly Durr, and the far flung community coordinators of The Great Books Foundation were exceedingly helpful in planning and executing the follow-up data collection. We also wish to thank the Foundation for its patience in letting social researchers have a go at them, not once, but twice.

In NORC, we could list dozens of names, but in particular we should like to thank Harold Levy and Sanford Abrams of our machine room staff; Joseph Zelan, virtuoso of the Monroe calculator; Selma Monsky and the entire field department of NORC, for their help in the field work; and Jean Johnson Arnold, who did the bulk of the coding.

Although it would not be obvious to anyone but a specialist in the field, a very large proportion of the ideas in this report follow from the work and advice of James S. Coleman, now of The Johns Hopkins University, and Peter Blau, of the University of Chicago.

In terms of the project staff, our division of labor was as follows. Ruth Ursula Gebhard had the sole responsibility for supervising the follow-up wave of data gathering and processing and is the author of Chapter Three, the bulk of which is reported in fuller detail in her master's thesis.[3] The study director edited her report for inclusion here, and any resultant distortions of the materials are not Miss Gebhard's fault. Herbert Hamilton analysed the individual level findings in Chapters Four, Five, and Six, and suggested a number of key interpretations for the analysis in all the chapters. Carolyn Huson did most of the calculations reported here, contributed very important ideas to the technical section of Chapter One, and was the analyst for the findings on the ef-

3. Ruth Ursula Gebhard, "Patterns of Participation Among Husbands and Wives in Discussion Groups," unpublished master's thesis (Chicago: Department of Sociology, University of Chicago, 1959).

fects of leadership and discussion techniques. Joe L. Spaeth, although not a regular member of the project team, is a co-author of the technical part of Chapter One. Since the rest of the report stands or falls on this methodological section, his contribution can not be measured in terms of hours alone. Although Lathrop Vickery Beale did not work on this part of the study, in several places we have lifted ideas and findings from the extensive analyses she has done during the life of this project. Charles S. Mack proofread the entire book and was extremely helpful in the editorial work.

Last, I should like to thank my wife, Martha Davis. Without her patience and perpetual coffee pot, this book would have been delayed even further beyond its original deadline.

None of these estimable people, however, has volunteered to shoulder the responsibility for errors of fact, method, interpretation, and English in the final draft of this volume, which has been prepared by the writer.

JAMES A. DAVIS

Chicago, Illinois
October, 1960

Contents

GREAT BOOKS
AND
SMALL GROUPS

1. *Problem and Method:*
Compositional Effects and the
Survival of Small Social Systems

Although this book is about
the dynamics of small groups, it does not fall neatly into the
classification, "group dynamics," or even the broader category
of "small groups" studies. In fact, the research really belongs
to that part of sociology known as comparative social structure. Although the social units we have studied are small
groups, the questions we asked and the analytical tools we
used led us away from the ideas associated with the small
group literature and toward concepts and variables generally
applied to the analysis of large scale societies.

§ The Decline and Fall
of Small Groups

The research question of our study is "Why do some groups
live and other groups die?" Because laboratory groups neither
live nor die, but continue at the pleasure of the experimenter,

this question has not been much studied in the tradition of experimental small groups research.

Philosophers and historians have long been fascinated by the search for an explanation of the rise and fall of societies. From Gibbon to Spengler to Toynbee and Sorokin bold minds have attempted to specify the reasons which can explain the decay or continuation of large scale social systems. More recently the structural functional theorists in sociology have considered this problem and have developed hypotheses at a rather high level of abstraction,[1] but despite a wealth of insights and ideas which have come from these broad-canvas approaches, the dynamics of large scale societies are still to be documented.

Shifting the scale of the problem from societies to small groups does little to improve the situation because as little is known about the survival of small social systems as is known about the future of Western civilization. About the only difference between the two problems is that many fewer people have worked on the latter; therefore, there are fewer answers which are known to be inadequate. This is so despite the fact that one of the most influential books in the small groups field claims that the small group is the most appropriate level for such studies. Homans writes:

> If we turn to history for help, it is astonishing how few societies have failed to survive. No doubt some primitive societies have disappeared, and all their members have died out, like the last of the Mohicans. But by far the more usual situation resembles the decline and fall of the Roman Empire. What fell then was not a society, but a governmental organization, an empire, whereas the society of Italy, for instance, survived the barbarian invasions, and has maintained

1. Cf. Talcott Parsons, *The Social System* (Glencoe, Ill.: The Free Press, 1951), pp. 26-36; David Aberle, A. K. Cohen, K. Davis, M. J. Levy, Jr., and F. X. Sutton, "The Functional Prerequisites of a Society," *Ethics*, IX (1950), 100-111; and Marion J. Levy, Jr., *The Structure of Society* (Princeton: Princeton Universty Press, 1952).

its continuity unbroken. . . . The meaning of social survival can be made much more precise for small units and organizations within a society than for the society itself. . . . In our own nation, small groups are breaking up every day, larger organizations dying from bankruptcy and other maladies. We have plenty of evidence with which to analyse their fitness to survive.[2]

If we define a decline and fall not as a change in institutional or cultural patterns but as a loosening of the social bonds so that many or all members cease interaction with each other, it would appear that small groups are indeed the natural unit for such studies, perhaps the only social organizations which suffer such a calamity. But despite Homans' optimism, as far as we can tell from a modest search of the literature, no one has made a quantitative comparative study of this problem at the level of the small group, unless one were to include the voluminous research on divorce. That is, we have been unable to find a study in which a number of non-family groups were followed over time and an attempt was made to see why some held their members and others lost them.

In short, we had both a practical and a theoretical interest in studying retention in our 172 discussion groups. From the viewpoint of Great Books (and this research was originally commissioned to aid in the operations of the program), retention is an important practical matter. To the extent that the program is able to maintain its groups, and maintain individuals in them, it will reach greater numbers of persons in a given year and its practical efficiency will increase. To the extent that groups disband or individuals leave their groups, the effectiveness of the program is lessened (our previous research indicated that for all of the effects meas-

2. George C. Homans, *The Human Group* (New York: Harcourt, Brace and Company, 1950), p. 270.

ured, changes increased steadily with length of exposure to the program) and costs of administration and organization rise.

From the viewpoint of social science, on the less practical side, data on retention provide unique information on factors involved in the survival of small social systems. Great Books groups are of particular interest to sociologists because they represent a sort of pure case. Perhaps the most striking characteristics of these groups are the properties which they do not have. Their leaders are not professional teachers, but volunteers recruited from the membership. Members pay no tuition, receive no diplomas, promotions, or merit badges for staying in. In fact, no one can complete the program, as additional readings are always available, currently up to the fourteenth year. The Great Books Foundation makes up the curriculum and sells the readings, but purchase of the readings is not required, and the foundation has little or no contact with a given group.

The upshot of all of this is that there are very few institutionalized pressures on a member to continue, since his "investment" is minimal and his tangible reward is nil. Although it is dangerous to compare natural groups with laboratory groups Great Books groups come pretty close to being pure discussion groups in which few variables other than the content of the program, the characteristics of a group's members, and the discussion process can affect the results. We should note, however, that this situation places severe limits on the generalization of our findings. Since almost all small groups—families, businesses, work groups, school rooms, etc.—are heavily shored up by the props of law, authority, and institution, there is no reason to believe that our findings can explain much about the dynamics of other types of groups. When we consider that a technical specialist, a lawyer, is usually necessary for the break up of a family, we must assume that our findings can not be applied willy nilly to all kinds of groups.

Being presented with a unique opportunity, we seized it and decided to follow Homans' advice and study the decline and fall not of societies, but of a sample of the social molecules which make up our society. However, we should not forget that the opportunity is unique.

§ Compositional Effects

If the dependent variable we have studied is an unusual one, so is our analysis of the independent ones. Rather than testing specific hypotheses, we have organized our research around a statistical method we call the analysis of "compositional effects." The method combines certain substantive questions about the nature of social influences with statistical techniques for assessing these influences. Because most of our report is based on compositional effect data, we shall here describe our method in some detail.

Let us assume that we have finally decided to pay off a mounting list of social obligations by throwing a party. Let us further assume that we have been so remiss in our obligations that, given our tiny apartment, we must have three separate parties. So, we sit down with the list of names and try to juggle them around so that things will work out well. Should we, for instance, try to make the three parties homogeneous—all people from the office at one, all neighbors at another, and, crossing our fingers, the parents of our children's school friends at the third? Or, should we try to mix the guests thoroughly and hope that chemistry, physiological or social, will generate a series of successful evenings?

The dilemma may appear trivial, except to the hostess, but it contains the germ of a very important problem—that of the relationships between individual characteristics and group characteristics. Our hesitation and indecision stems from a tacit assumption that groups are real, and that there is something to group situations beyond that accounted for by adding up the characteristics of the individuals involved. Thus, to have one amateur pianist at the party may help a lot, but to have four may not be so desirable. On the other hand, if we invite *only* amateur pianists, they may have a marvelous time discussing music.

While the general problem of the relations between groups and individuals has been vigorously discussed for some 2500 years, that particular corner of it which was suggested by our party problem, has received little attention in social science. Actually, it is a practical problem which turns up rather frequently in modern society. Should, for instance, school children be grouped according to their abilities, or mixed up randomly? Do the modern suburbs, which are so homogeneous in their class structure and family type, produce stultifying effects on the children who grow up there? What are the optimal proportions of whites and Negroes to maintain a stable inter-racial neighborhood? Or again: should older, retired people be advised to live with their families or should they be segregated into homogeneous colonies of people with similar interests and problems? Does coeducation lead to greater or lesser concentration on studies? And finally, are there any general rules which would help us in making up small, informal discussion groups, in such a way as to maximize the quality of the discussions?

Each of these queries really asks, in a particular situation, the same general question: Given people who possess some particular characteristic, will they behave differently in groups which vary in the proportion having that characteristic?

Contemporary sociology is quite interested in this problem —which we can call the "compositional problem," but the issues involved may be clearer if we begin with the great pioneer sociologist, Emile Durkheim, and his 1895 essay, *The Rules of Sociological Method*.[3]

3. E. Durkheim, *The Rules of Sociological Method* (1895, eighth edition), translated by S. A. Solovay and J. H. Mueller, and edited by G. E. G. Catlin (Glencoe, Illinois: The Free Press, 1950).

Durkheim begins by asking what sorts of phenomena are peculiarly social, and hence, whether sociology has a unique domain of study. In particular he is faced with the challenge of discriminating between "individual" and "social" events. His answer is that social facts "are not only external to the individual but are, moreover, endowed with coercive power, by virtue of which they impose themselves upon him, independent of his individual will." In his essay, Durkheim defends his position with a number of verbal examples, for instance, "When I fulfill my obligations as brother, husband, or citizen, when I execute my contracts, I perform duties which are defined, externally to myself and my acts, in law and in custom."

When, however, one turns to statistical data, in the fashion of contemporary sociology, it is difficult to deduce what properties should appear in a set of observations if they are to be in accordance with Durkheim's strictures. This question can be broken into two separate problems: the problem of assessing constraint and the problem of assessing exteriority. Constraint presents little difficulty, since Durkheim stresses that the constraint need not be perceived ("If the complacency with which we permit ourselves to be carried along conceals the pressure undergone, nevertheless it does not abolish it. Thus, the air is no less heavy because we do not detect its weight.") All that one needs to demonstrate constraint is a correlation between an exterior situation and a behavior. Thus, although the heavy stress in Durkheim's analysis is on normative constraint, he includes by implication relationships based on the existence of laws of behavior as well as those deriving from social norms.

The empirical assessment of "exteriority" is another matter. When he is discussing examples of exteriority Durkheim typically cites cultural phenomena such as codes of law, business rules, and religious systems, which exist as symbols independent of particular persons. However, to limit social facts to the realm of culture would exclude inter-personal

phenomena from sociology and do an injustice to the spirit
of Durkheim's work. Frequently, the exterior social fact is a
person or group of persons, so that the same empirical phe-
nomenon can be simultaneously individual fact and exterior
social fact.

Durkheim wrestled with the statistical problems implied
by this position, and although he usually managed to reach
correct statistical answers in advance of the historical development of statistics, this time he failed. He wrote:

> Currents of opinion . . . impel certain groups either to
> more marriages, for example, or to more suicides, or to a
> higher or lower birth-rate, etc. These currents are plainly
> social facts. At first sight they seem inseparable from the
> forms they take in individual cases. But statistics furnish us
> with the means of isolating them. They are, in fact, repre-
> sented with considerable exactness by the rates of births,
> marriages, and suicides. . . . Since each of these figures con-
> tains all the individual cases indiscriminately, the individual
> circumstances which may have had a share in the production
> of the phenomena are neutralized.

Perhaps the difficulty lies in two senses of the word "individual." If it means "unique circumstances of a particular
person," one would expect that averages based on large numbers of cases would (by definition) be unaffected by them.
However, if it means personal characteristics as opposed to
characteristics of an exterior social system, it is not clear that
averages always represent social facts. For instance, the finding that Catholic communities have lower average suicide
rates than Protestant communities may reflect some property
of Catholic communities (a social fact exterior to the individual members of the communities), or it may reflect some
propensity of individual Catholics and Protestants which is
not necessarily a social fact in Durkheim's sense. The finding
is consistent with any of the following inferences: 1) Catho-

lics are less likely to commit suicide regardless of the religious composition of the community. 2) In communities with many Catholics, both Catholics and Protestants are less likely to commit suicide, but within a given community there is no religious difference in suicide rates. 3) Catholics are *more* likely to to commit suicide than are Protestants, but both religions have lower suicide rates where there are many Catholics. 4) In each community, Catholics have the same suicide rate, but the suicide rate of Protestants declines with the proportion of Catholics. All these statements assert some sort of relationship between religion and suicide, but they differ widely in their substantive implications about social and individual factors because they differ in their assumptons about the nature of the effect at the individual level (religious differences in a given community) and the group level (differences between persons of the same religion in different communities).

The general conclusion is that from a correlation between averages (or proportions) one can not tell much about whether there is a group level difference, an individual level difference, or both. The statistical principle underlying these ambiguities has been recognized for some time. One aspect of it has been stated as "the fallacy of ecological correlation" [4] which states that one may not necessarily infer individual level correlations from group level relationships. Patricia Kendall and Paul F. Lazarsfeld, however, in analyzing methodological problems in *The American Soldier,* suggest that the principle can lead to positive gains if the data allow for simultaneous group and individual level analyses. They write:

> There is no reason why unit data cannot be used to characterize individuals in the unit. A man who does not have malaria in a unit where the incidence of malaria is very low

4. William S. Robinson, "Ecological Correlations and the Behavior of Individuals," *American Sociological Review,* XV (1950)), 351-357.

probably feels differently about his state of health than does the man who has no malaria but serves in a unit with high incidence. . . .

In terms of actual analysis the matter can be restated in the following terms: just as we can classify people by demographic variables or by their attitudes, we can also classify them by the kind of environment in which they live. The appropriate variables for such a classification are likely to be unit data. A survey analysis would then cover both personal and unit data simultaneously.[5]

Since then a number of students and colleagues of Kendall and Lazarsfeld have seized upon this approach as a research strategy. Thus, Berelson, Lazarsfeld, and McPhee show that among friendship groups the per cent voting Republican increases with the proportion in the group whose party affiliation is Republican, both among individuals whose party affiliation is Republican and for those who are Democrats.[6] Or again, Lipset, Trow, and Coleman[7] in their study of the I. T. U. report that in shops where there is consensus on politics, political interest is higher (regardless of political preference) than in shops where there is a division in political allegiance.

Such findings are, of course, not new. Durkheim himself in his work on suicide noted not only that suicide rates vary considerably among different religions, but also that for a given religion suicide rates are much lower when its adherents are in a distinct minority in the society.[8] Groves and

5. P. L. Kendall and P. F. Lazarsfeld, "Problems of Survey Analysis," in R. K. Merton and P. F. Lazarsfeld (eds.), *Continuities in Social Research: Studies in the Scope and Method of 'The American Soldier'* (Glencoe, Illinois: The Free Press, 1950), pp. 195-196.

6. B. R. Berelson, P. F. Lazarsfeld, and W. N. McPhee, *Voting: A Study of Opinion Formation in a Presidential Campaign* (Chicago, Illinois: University of Chicago Press, 1954), pp. 100-101.

7. S. M. Lipset, M. A. Trow, and J. S. Coleman, *Union Democracy* (Glencoe, Illinois: The Free Press, 1956), pp. 163-171.

8. E. Durkheim, *Suicide, A Study in Sociology* (1897). Translated by J. A. Spaulding and G. Simpson (Glencoe, Illinois: The Free Press, 1951).

Ogburn, in a book published in 1928[9] show that the marriage rates for men and women vary in opposite directions with the sex ratios of the communities in which they live. Similarly, Faris and Dunham, in their 1939 study of the ecological distribution of home addresses of psychotics in Chicago, found that some psychosis rates were higher for Negroes living in white areas and whites living in Negro areas than for the same races when living in areas where they comprised the majority.[10] And, of course, a number of findings in *The American Soldier* were of this type, including the ever-cited analysis which showed that while promoted soldiers were less critical of the military promotion system than non-promoted soldiers, criticism was greater among both promoted and non-promoted in units with high rates of promotion.[11]

In an article published in 1957, Peter Blau called such relationships "structural effects" and defined them as follows.

> The general principle is that if ego's X affects not only ego's Y but also alter's Y, a structural effect will be observed, which means that the distribution of X in a group is related to Y even though the individual's X is held constant. Such a finding indicates that the network of relations in the group with respect to X influences Y. It isolates the effects of X on Y that are entirely due to or transmitted by the process of social interaction.[12]

Our analysis stems from the ideas advanced by the Columbia University group, and differs only as follows. First,

9. Ernest R. Groves and William F. Ogburn, *American Marriage and Family Relationships* (New York: Henry Holt and Company, 1928), pp. 193-205.

10. R. E. L. Faris and H. W. Dunham, *Mental Disorders in Urban Areas* (Chicago: The University of Chicago Press, 1939), pp. 110-123.

11. S. A. Stouffer, *Studies in Social Psychology in World War II*, Vol. 1, *The American Soldier During Army Life* (Princeton, New Jersey: Princeton University Press, 1949).

12. P. M. Blau, "Formal Organization: Dimensions of Analysis," *American Journal of Sociology*, LXIII (1957), 64.

we shall call these phenomena "compositional" rather than "structural" effects because we think there is only a partial overlap between these relationships and what sociologists consider to be social structure. Second, we shall suggest some simple formal procedures for statistical analysis. Third, rather than considering merely individual effects *versus* group effects, we shall suggest a typology of possible relationships.

§ Procedures

In order to make the shift from essentially verbal analysis to concrete statistical operations, we shall have to begin with a brief set of definitions and notations.

Let us consider two or more populations or groups, which we shall denote with arabic numerals. Within each population, individuals may be characterized by the presence or absence of a given *independent* attribute (A or $\bar{A}$). Consequently, each population may be characterized by the proportion of its members having the attribute, which is also the probability that a member selected at random is an "A." Kendall and Lazarsfeld refer to such a group level datum as a rate.[13] We shall denote these rates or probabilities as P_1, P_2, P_3, etc., the subscript designating the population in question. Within each of the populations we can also determine the probability that a member of a subclass defined by the presence or absence of A possesses a given *dependent* attribute. Thus, we shall define D_{A1} as the probability that an A in population$_1$ possesses the dependent attribute. Finally, the probability that any unselected member of a specific group possesses the dependent attribute will be denoted by D_1, D_2, D_3, etc.[14]

13. P. L. Kendall and P. F. Lazarsfeld, *op. cit.*, p. 191.

14. While we shall limit our exposition to attribute data, there is no reason in principle why this technique can not be applied to data characterized by more sophisticated forms of measurement. Thus, the D value could be a mean or a median. If, however, the P values are means, our classification of types of relationships does not necessarily apply.

The underlying strategy of any such analysis consists of making comparisons between the *D* probabilities in different categories. In our situation, there are two basic axes of comparison: (a) We may compare members of a particular group who belong to different subclasses of the independent attribute and (b) we may compare members of the same subclass who belong to different groups. The end result will be a set of probability or percentage differences, one set of *within group differences* and a second set of *between group differences*.

A hypothetical example may make these distinctions clearer. Let us assume that we have conducted a survey in four different communities and are investigating the relationship between religion and egoism, following Durkheim. The results of this hypothetical study are presented in the following fictitious table.

Table 1.1—Hypothetical Survey Findings

City and Religion	Egoistic (per cent)	N
Oneville:		
Protestant	77	600
Catholic	43	400
Twoville:		
Protestant	68	400
Catholic	32	600
Threeville:		
Protestant	59	200
Catholic	21	800
N-ville:		
Protestant	86	800
Catholic	54	200

Table 1 can be described in the terminology outlined above as follows:

$D = $ The per cent suffering from egoism (e.g., 59 per cent among Protestants in Threeville)

$A = $ Protestant

$\bar{A} = $ Catholic

$P = $ The per cent of the town which is Protestant (e.g., 20 per cent in Threeville)

Thus, D_{A2} is the per cent egoistic among Catholics in community$_2$ (32 per cent); D_{A1} is the per cent egoistic among Protestants in community$_1$ (77 per cent).

Let us now make the two types of comparisons. Within each community, when we compare Catholics and Protestants, we find that Protestants are more likely to be egoistic than Catholics. Then, when we compare Protestants in different communities, we notice a range of values (77-68-59-86), as we also do when we compare Catholics in different communities (43-32-21-54).

We conclude that within each community there is a difference related to religion, and between communities there are differences among people of the same religion. Have we then demonstrated a compositional effect? Not quite, for we haven't shown that the inter-community differences are associated with variation in community population composition. Thus, we definitely see some sort of "contextual effect," but until we rearrange the communities in order according to their P values, we haven't shown that the inter-community differences *vary with* compositional variation. To put it formally:

A compositional effect exists when the absolute value of either (a) the within group difference and/or (b) the between group difference for A's and/or Ā's can be described as a function of P.

One way of doing this is to shift from a percentage table to a graph in which the vertical axis is the D probability, the horizontal axis is P, and the points are the D values for the subclasses in the populations considered. Chart 1.1 illustrates the graph for our hypothetical survey.

Chart 1.1 being fictitious, is nice and clear. Examining it carefully, we note the following.

a. Among both the A's (solid line) and the $\bar{A}$'s (dotted line) there is a linear increase of D as P increases.

b. The two lines connecting the observations are parallel.

Chart 1.1
Graph of Hypothetical Compositional Effect

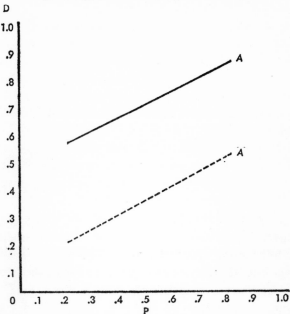

From these two observations, we can make the following inferences about our hypothetical compositional effect.

a. There is a distinct compositional effect on the between group difference, for among both A's and $\bar{A}$'s D increases steadily with P; hence, variation in the social composition produces an effect on behavior even when the individual attribute is controlled.

b. There is no compositional effect on the within group difference, for at all P levels the difference between D_A and $D_{\bar{A}}$ is constant; hence, variation in the social composition produces no effect on behavior within a group, other than that accounted for by the individual level difference common throughout the universe.

As often happens when one proceeds to formalize a verbal

statement, the possibilities turn out to be more numerous than expected. Thus, it appears that there can be at least two rather different types of compositional effects, one a change in the between group differences and the other a change in the within group difference, as *P* varies. Since, in addition, the lines need not be straight, it is clear that potentially, at least, instead of "one" compositional effect, there can be a rather wide variety of types. In the following section, we shall present a classification of types of compositional effects.

§ A Classification of Compositional Effects

When we defined compositional effects as functions, we were careful to set no limitation on the kind of function involved, but merely stated that such effects will be recognized whenever one or both of our differences varies with *P*. Thus, there is no reason, in principle, why compositional effects could not take the form of any of the luxuriant spirals and curves which thrive in mathematics texts.

Nevertheless, even in preliminary work with a technique, some attempt at classification will aid in structuring the analysis. Therefore, we will suggest that out of the infinite possibilities, eight loom in strategic importance. Our classification system combines some elementary mathematical considerations with some speculations about the social processes which might generate the mathematical forms.

Let us begin with the mathematics. One of the attractive features of compositional analysis is that in the process qualitative data are transmuted into quantitative data. That is, even though *A* is an attribute or qualitative observation, *P* can be treated as a real number. It has a meaningful zero point, the distances between *P* values can be given real numbers, and the values may legitimately be squared. Given this property, it is possible to describe the functions by which compositional effects are defined in terms of the standard geometrical analogues of algebraic equations—linear, monotonic, parabolic, etc.

Now, let us consider the possible effects of *A* on *D*.

1) The attribute can increase or decrease the probability of *D*, regardless of *P*. This is the individual level difference.

2) *P* can influence the probability of *D* among *A*'s and *Ā*'s equally. This is the group level difference.

3) There can be an interaction in the effects. Although they are logically equivalent, there are two different ways of describing this. First, one may say that *P* influences the probability of *D*, but differentially for the *A*'s and *Ā*'s. We can think of this as "differential susceptibility," since such relationships suggest that *A*'s and *Ā*'s differ in their reactions to variation in composition. Alternatively, we can say that *A* can increase or decrease the probability of *D*, but differentially at different *P* levels. We can think of this as "conditional individual differences" since such relationships suggest that the size of the individual level effect is contingent upon the group composition. Such interactions are neither group level differences nor individual level differences, but a combination of the two. If individual differences are analogous to Durkheim's individual facts, and group level differences are analogous to Durkheim's social facts, perhaps we can think of these interactions as social-psychological facts.

What should our graphs show for these three kinds of effects?

a. If there is an individual level effect operating, some of the parameters of the functions for the *A*'s and *Ā*'s will differ, and, geometrically, they will be described by two distinct lines or curves. If there is no such process operating, the functions for the *A*'s and *Ā*'s will be identical, and, geometrically, there will be only one line, regardless of whether or not there is a group level effect.

b. If there is a group level effect, *P* or a function of *P* will be a parameter for the *A*'s and *Ā*'s, and, geometrically, both of the lines will depart from a straight line parallel to the *P* axis. If there is no such effect, both lines will be parallel to the *P* axis.

c. If the third type of effect occurs, *P* or a power of *P* will be a parameter in the functions, but *P* will have different values for *A*'s and *Ā*'s. Graphically, there will be two lines or curves which are not parallel.

We are now ready to examine the specific types of compositional effects. Let us begin by dividing the possibilities into two large groups: first, the linear cases, in which the equations describing *D* as a function of *P* do not involve powers of *P* greater or less than one, and hence can be plotted with a straight line, and second, the cases in which one or more of the functions is not linear.

Chart 1.2 summarizes the five basic possibilities in the linear case. Within each cell we have placed a graph illustrating the geometrical results. In all our graphs we shall follow these conventions: (a) The vertical axis is the probability of *D* from 0 to 1.00; (b) The horizontal axis is the value of *P* from 0 to 1.00; (c) The solid line connects points representing *D* values among the *A*'s for particular *P* values; (d) The dotted line connects points representing *D* values among the *Ā*'s, for particular *P* values.

Let us consider each of the five types in turn.

Type 0.—Type 0 is a trivial case. Both *A* and *Ā* produce the same horizontal line running parallel to the *P* axis. In type 0, *A* has no effect on *D* whatsoever. There is no individual level difference, no between groups difference, and no difference of the third type.

Type I.—In a type I relationship we find two horizontal lines, parallel to each other and to the *P* axis. This means that at every level of *P* there is a within group difference between *A*'s and *Ā*'s, and this difference is constant, the relationship being interpreted as what we have called a pure individual level effect.

Type II.—A type II relationship is the polar opposite of

Chart 1.2
Classification of Relationships for the Linear Case

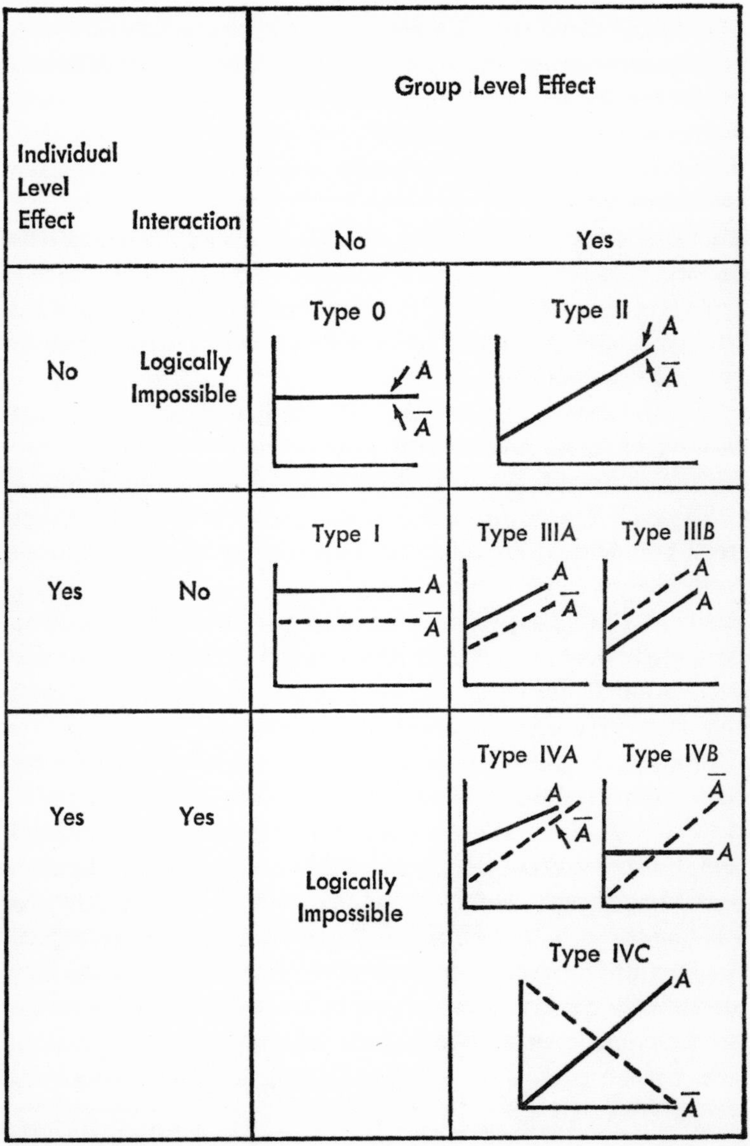

Individual Level Effect	Interaction	Group Level Effect	
		No	Yes
No	Logically Impossible	Type 0	Type II
Yes	No	Type I	Type IIIA Type IIIB
Yes	Yes	Logically Impossible	Type IVA Type IVB Type IVC

type I, corresponding to a "pure" group effect in which we observe a between groups difference related to P, but no within group difference at all. The end result is a single straight line for both A's and $\bar{A}$'s, as illustrated in Chart 2.

Type II relationships present some interesting problems for interpretation. The influence process here may be thought of as acting in the absence of any individual trait difference. The effect may possibly be thought of as "catalytic" in which the influence of the attribute works through affecting the group climate or milieu without influencing individuals directly.

Type IIIA.—In a type III relationship we see a combination of type I and type II. That is, there is a constant individual difference, along with a linear effect of group composition. In Chart 2, we see that the graphic representation of such an effect consists of two parallel lines which rise or fall with P. Substantively it suggests a sort of band wagon effect.

Type IIIB.—Type IIIB is the same as type IIIA, except for a paradoxical fact, the individual level effect is opposite from the group level effect.[15] In Chart 1.2, we see an example where, within groups, being an A leads to lower D probabilities, while between groups, the proportion of A's leads to an increase in D among both subclasses. One would think that this is merely one of those unlikely things ground out by listing logical possibilities, except that this is the model for the classic Air Force—Military Police finding: Within units, promoted soldiers are more pleased with the promotion system, but between units, the proportion who approve declines with the per cent promoted, among both types of soldiers. As Blau notes in his discussion of structural effects, such phenomena are extremely important for the sociologist as they are striking confirmations of his claim that group level effects are different from individual level effects.

15. A formal theory which purports to explain one Type IIIB effect has been suggested by one of the writers. Cf. James A. Davis, "A Formal Interpretation of the Theory of Relative Deprivation," *Sociometry*, XXII (1959), 280-296.

Type IV.—Type IV relationships consist of those forms where there are two straight lines which are not parallel. This corresponds to what we have called differential susceptibility or conditional individual differences. The difference in slope of the two lines can be interpreted as a differential suscepti-bility to the process for the A's and the $\bar{A}$'s, or as change in the individual level correlation. Since there are many ways in which lines can diverge, there are obviously many different kinds of type IV relationships. In Chart 1.2, however, we have selected three which are of interest. In example IVA, we see a situation where both groups show a linear increase with P, but the rate of increase, or slope, of the line is greater for one group (here, the $\bar{A}$'s) than for the other. That is, in the example, the $\bar{A}$'s are more sensitive to variation in composi-tion than the A's. In type IVB, we find the A line parallel to the P axis, and the $\bar{A}$ line showing a linear increase. This sug-gests that only the $\bar{A}$'s are sensitive to composition, while the A's are immune to its effect. Finally, in type IVC, we see a situation where both groups show approximately the same amount of effect, but the direction of the effect is reversed. That is, the D rate increases with P for one group and de-creases for the other. Actually, a type IV relationship is not as esoteric as it appears, for it may simply be interpreted as saying that for each group D is a linear function of its ma-jority-minority position.

In spite of their obvious differences, all the type IV linear relationships share one property: in each the *percentage dif-ference* between the A's and the $\bar{A}$'s is a linear function of P. That is, the individual level correlation varies directly as a function of P. In types IVA and IVB the correlation main-tains direction, but varies in magnitude, and in the case of IVC, we find a reversal of the sign of the correlation.

This completes our description of the five major linear forms. We have been unable to provide a complete codifica-tion of the non-linear types, but we shall sketch out some which deserve specific, although brief, discussions.

In certain cases the forms which appear will not be linear, but will show a definite direction. Technically speaking, we can call them monotonic functions and include among them all forms in which the graph is not linear, but where the resultant curves never rise *and* fall. Step functions, in which for certain ranges of P there is no effect, but at others there is a precipitous rise; accelerating and decelerating curves, and certain combinations of the two would be included here. Chart 1.3 illustrates some *a priori* possibilities.

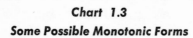

Chart 1.3
Some Possible Monotonic Forms

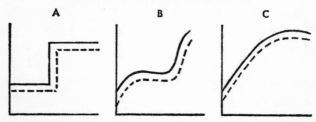

Example *a* illustrates a step-function, which would suggest that there is some threshold necessary before the compositional influence effect occurs. In example *b* we see a situation where the rate of change is greater at the extremes than in the middle of the range, which in terms of an influence model would suggest a situation where the influence process was most effective when one of the groups of "influencers" was clearly dominant, a situation sometimes suggested in propaganda and communications research. The final example, *c*, is simply a case where D increases at a decreasing rate with increase in P, a situation which substantively suggests something like a saturation process.

Monotonic forms may in addition include any of the basic types of relationships as we have defined them for the linear cases, all of the examples in Chart 1.3 being type IIIA.

A second type of non-linear compositional effect is one in which the curves produced have a single mode or peak, that is, where the curve describing the relationship has a single bend, the general family of parabolas being a good example. Substantively, they suggest either an "optimum" point or the result of consensus. Thus, for instance, if (as in the example cited from *Union Democracy*) sheer unanimity were important for the occurrence of D, we should expect to find that the D levels at extremely high or low P values would be identical, but that the curve would reach a minimum around .5 where heterogeneity is highest.

§ Techniques of Analysis

The considerations advanced above suggest that the basic technique for the analysis of compositional effects is standard bivariate regression and covariance analysis. However, there are difficult problems concerning N's and degrees of freedom are knotty with these data, and the general strategy of analysis is worth discussing.

Let us begin with the general approach. We assume that in any practical research situation, either the data will be a probability sample or, if a universe, will never fit any of the model forms suggested without some degree of error. Therefore, the basic question in compositional analysis is not "What form is it?", but rather, "To what form are the data a reasonable approximation?" We suggest that the null hypotheses implied are: (a) These data could have been sampled from a universe in which there is no compositional effect and (b) if null hypothesis (a) must be rejected, these data could have been sampled from a universe in which the effect is mathematically least complicated.

These two considerations suggest that the natural steps in such analyses are as follows.

1) Fitting the best possible straight line for the A's and also for the $\bar{A}$'s, using the least squares criterion.

2) If the null hypothesis of linearity cannot be rejected,

testing the departure of the slope(s) from zero, testing for a difference in slopes, and testing whether the lines, if "parallel" are significantly different in intercept.

3) If the null hypothesis of linearity is rejected, testing the fit of successively more complicated functions until a reasonable fit is achieved or analysis is abandoned.

The computational approach is that of standard textbook procedures for regression and covariance, but a knotty problem arises when one considers the problem of N, the number of observations to be used in the calculations. If more than one element is sampled from a given collectivity, the sample is heavily clustered, and the effective sample size is much less than the number of individuals sampled. On the other hand, if individuals are selected independently within collectivities, the effective sample size is greater than the number of groups, although smaller than the number of individuals. Handbooks of sampling statistics do provide formulas for such situations, but our practical experience has been that the calculations are too involved and expensive to make them useful in survey situations where a large number of tests are being made. Our current convention is to proceed as if N is equivalent to the number of aggregates, but this is a conservative convention and is wasteful of data. In any set of data, there is, of course, more than one way of forming such aggregates. Either we can use the natural units (e.g. each of our discussion groups) or one can aggregate data on the basis of grouped P values. If the data are grouped into deciles, N will be 10. This is the convention we used in our analysis, and it undoubtedly increased our chances of making type II errors. However, we felt that in exploratory research which is subject to the biases of searching around for relationships, such conservatism was justified.

§ Summary

This book is a study of small groups of a type similar to those studied in the social science laboratory. Although they are natural groups, they essentially consist of a small number of volunteers who meet to discuss topics assigned to them by outsiders. However, our study differs from most small groups research in two important ways. First, the dependent variable is not the structure or pattern of interaction of the group at a given time, but rather its loss or retention of membership over a period of one year. Although such a "decline and fall" research problem is usually treated in terms of whole societies or institutions—following the suggestion of Homans, we have concluded that natural small groups are a particularly appropriate source of data on this problem. Second, our analysis is centered on a statistical device which enables us to ask a particular question about each variable in the study: "Does it affect membership retention through individual level effects or by creating a group composition which is favorable or unfavorable for holding members?" In this chapter the research problem has been sketched and the statistical technique described in some detail. We are now ready to turn to a description of the people in Great Books and then to a description of the roles they play in the discussions, and finally to an analysis of how people and roles as individual and group properties affect the survival of these groups.

2. The People in Great Books Groups

Most small groups studies are based on data from university undergraduates or soldiers, traditional, but unrepresentative samples of the range of human possibilities. Although our study is based on a national probability sample instead of volunteers or draftees, Great Books members are not just plain folks, but a highly selected group of people. In order to evaluate the findings of our study, it is necessary to keep in mind the sort of people we have studied. Two separate questions arise here. First, we shall note the ways in which our respondents were selected from the universe of Great Books members. Second, and more important, we shall note, within the limits of the information available to us, the ways in which Great Books members are selected from the general American population.

§ The Sample

During December, 1957, NORC interviewers attended the regular meetings of 172 groups. Members had not been informed before the meeting that they were to participate in the research that night, although some knew that their group would be called on at some time. Previous arrangements had been made with the group leaders who had agreed not to inform their members of the date questionnaires were to be administered.

Each member of the sampled groups filled out a 32 page self-administered questionnaire. By and large, we found co-operation to be good. Although a number of groups were visibly disappointed that they had to forego their discussions, only one protocol was rejected because inspection indicated that the writer did not give serious cooperation. One other schedule, from a member whose physical handicap resulted in an illegible questionnaire, was excluded, leaving a total of 1,909 cases from 172 groups.

The questionnaires were coded and punched onto IBM cards for analysis. Although we do have some informal reports by the NORC interviewers, the materials presented here are based on statistical analyses of these cards.

Our sample is a stratified (by year of reading) probability sample of the Great Books discussion groups which in November and December, 1957, were meeting in NORC "primary sampling units." Since each member of the sampled groups was asked to fill out a schedule, the number of individuals each group contributed to the total sample was obviously proportional to its size; hence, our sample is also representative of "individuals" as well as groups, although this procedure results in the sample of individuals being heavily clustered.

NORC is set up to take probability samples of the general population of the United States. In order to do so, it maintains a permanent field staff of trained interviewers in a national sample of counties and standard metropolitan areas. These are known as "primary sampling units." The counties were selected in such a way that by weighting the interviews, national estimates for a cross section of the general population are efficiently and accurately obtained, subject, of course, to random sampling error.

For technical reasons which are inherent in any such sample drawn by any research agency, bias is introduced when one attempts to sample a universe with a relatively small number of individuals such as Great Books groups. The net effect of this bias is that while the cases sampled are representative of cases in their type of county in the country, too many cases are drawn from large cities and too few cases are drawn from small towns and rural areas.

Our sample of Great Books groups, consequently, has too many cases from large cities and too few cases from small cities. We knew this would happen when we began the study, but chose to use the method we did for the following reasons.

1) The Great Books program itself is disproportionately urban. Thus, in 1955, the last year for which NORC had complete data on the program available, the standard metropolitan areas of the United States, which included 56 per cent of the U.S. 1950 population, had 75 per cent of the Great Books groups.

2) Our budget precluded the use of trained interviewers for a true national sample, and we felt that it was preferable to have national coverage, even with an urban bias, rather than to have perfect sampling of a limited geographical area such as the midwest.

In the fall of 1957 we listed all of the groups in NORC sample points which were registered with the Great Books Foundation. (A few groups may have lost contact with the Foundation and hence may have been excluded from the universe.) The listed groups were stratified by year of reading and the following proportions were taken in each stratum, with the aim of netting 50 first year groups, 30 each in years II through IV, and 30 in years V or more.

Of the 182 groups drawn, 164 were surveyed without any further ado. However, 18 groups presented special problems: Five did not meet during the field period, five were defunct,

Table 2.1—Distribution of Groups in NORC PSU'S by Stratum

Year of Reading	N	Sampling Proportion
I	233	.25
II	122	.33
III	96	.33
IV	52	.60
V and higher	93	.33
Not recorded on registration card	33	.33

four were groups in another program administered by the Foundation or had participated in the pre-test or were duplicates of sampled groups, two had split into two new groups each, one repeatedly postponed the questionnaire session beyond the field work deadline, and one leader refused.

In the case of the two groups which had reproduced by cell division, all four sections were interviewed and counted as separate groups. Of the other 16, four were replaced with a random selection from the proper stratum at the same sample point. For the remaining 12, either the stratum was exhausted or the difficulty turned up so late in the field work period that there was no time for replacement.

The "take rate" we achieved is well within the norms for survey research, and we may conclude that we ended up with a representative sample of groups from our NORC primary sampling units. Our urban disproportion, however, remains, for the reasons noted above.

Of course, for a variable which is not related to city size, this bias is unimportant. In order to find out which variables might be affected by this sampling problem, we divided the respondents into the following groups.

1) Those living within the city limits of Central Cities of a Standard Metropolitan Area of one million or more (303 cases).

2) Those living within the city limits of Central Cities of a Standard Metropolitan Area of 250,000 to 999,999 ($N = 526$).

3) Those living within 20 miles of the city limits of the

Central City of a Standard Metropolitan Area, in a city with a population of 25,000 to 250,000 ($N = 231$).

4) Those living within 20 miles of the city limits of a Central City of a Standard Metropolitan Area, in a city with a population of 10,000 to 24,999 ($N = 204$).

5) Those living within 20 miles of the city limits of a Central City of Standard Metropolitan Area, in a city with a population under 10,000 ($N = 315$).

6) Those living more than 20 miles from the city limits of the Central City of a Standard Metropolitan Area, in a city of 25,000 or less ($N = 256$).

7) All other ($N = 32$).

We can think of these types as follows: 1) Very large cities; 2) Large cities; 3) Large suburbs and satellite cities; 4) Medium suburbs and satellite cities; 5) Small suburbs and satellite cities; and 6) Small towns.[1]

We compared the social characteristics of respondents from these six types and found no consistent differences in:

1) Age

2) Education

3) Feeling that the program has had a high impact

4) Scores on a test of knowledge of liberal arts and humanities

5) Self-definition as "intellectual" or "non-intellectual"

6) Interest in community affairs

Table 2.2 summarizes the differences we find.

The first three "biases" do not appear to be too important, but we thought they should be on record. There is a slight tendency for there to be greater proportions of men, lower status heads of households, and advanced year participants in the small towns.

The three important differences are these.

1) Jews are less frequent in the smaller towns than in the

1. We should stress that the classification is crude. A number of Standard Metropolitan Areas extend more than 20 miles beyond the core city. However, we hope that our classification will give us some perspective on the problem.

Table 2.2—Social Characteristics and Community

VARIABLE	CITY			SUBURB		SMALL TOWN
	Very Large	Large	Large	Medium	Small	
Female	65%	63%	64%	61%	68%	55%
High occupational status of head of household	29	36	37	40	43	24
Zero years of Great Books completed	39	50	39	43	40	34
Jewish	34	10	20	12	8	11
Married	62	66	80	86	87	91
Republican	23	37	43	52	50	52

large urban areas (this being true in general, as well as in Great Books).

2) Republicans are more frequent in smaller towns.

3) Married participants are more frequent in smaller towns.

In summary, our sample was planned to overestimate the proportion of advanced year members; for technical reasons it was forced to overestimate the proportion from larger communities; and as a result of the community size effect, it overestimates the proportions of Jews, Democrats, and non-married people in the program. We do not believe that these biases are serious, and, where necessary, account is taken for the biases in our interpretations.

§ Member Characteristics

What are they like? What sorts of people are attracted to Great Books? We shall attempt to describe the 1,909 participants in our sample in terms of their salient social characteristics—education, family situation, occupation, self-conceptions, religious preference, and political party preference. We have no data on their secret dreams and hidden motives, but we do have the basic bricks from which to build a sociological description of the members in terms of the roles which they play in their families, communities, and the larger society, and their reported motives for joining Great Books.

When we say "What are they like?" we usually mean "How are they different?", which, in turn, raises the question of "different from whom?" It is hardly necessary to document the ways in which 1,909 adult Americans differ from, say, 1,909 adult Chinese. What we would really like to know is how the people in Great Books differ from other people in their communities who had an opportunity to join, but did not. Thus, the question we raise really implies the necessity of having data from a control sample of people who might have been in the program, but are not. We have no such data in our study, but here and there we can contrast our materials with published findings. The differences we find can be at best suggestive, given the methodological problems involved, but in this chapter we shall note them.

Perhaps the most striking characteristic of the members is their high level of formal education. In the following table they are compared with 1950 Census data on the total U.S. population 25 years of age and over.

Table 2.3—Educational Attainment

Education	Number of Participants	Per Cent of Participants	Per Cent of U.S. Adult Population 1950
No college	297	16	86
Part college	433	24	7
Bachelor's degree	414	23 ⎫	6
Graduate study	682	37 ⎭	
	1,826	100	99
(No answer and uncodeable)	83		
	1,909		

The contrast is plain. Eighty-four per cent of the participants have had at least some college, while 86 per cent of the total population have had none. Our sample even includes 100 Ph.D.s, who make up five per cent of the sample, while Ph.D.s account for roughly one-tenth of one per cent of the general population.

This high educational level is not shared equally by the sexes. Men report higher educational attainments as is shown in Table 2.4.[2]

Table 2.4—Educational Attainment by Sex

Education	Men	Women
No college	9%	21%
Part college	16	28
Bachelor's	21	24
Graduate work	54	27
	100%	100%
N	682	1,133

More than half of the men have graduate work beyond the bachelor's degree and 91 per cent have some college training. Among the women the percentages are less, but we still note that half (51 per cent) of the women are college graduates.

Thus, it is perhaps fair to characterize Great Books as a program for, and almost limited to, "college people," the majority of whom have a bachelor's degree, and a considerable proportion of whom report graduate work or degrees beyond the bachelor's.

In order to assess the ways in which the participants view themselves subjectively, we asked them the following question.

Which of the following comes closest to the way you think about yourself?

1_____ I don't like the phrase particularly, but I guess you'd have to call me an "intellectual."

2_____ I consider myself an educated person, but not really an "intellectual."

3_____ I haven't had too much education, so I can't really call myself either an "intellectual" or an "educated person," but I am pretty serious in my approach to things.

2. *N* refers to the bases on which the percentages were calculated. Where *N*'s differ from table to table, it is due to non-response on one or more items in the table.

4——— I guess I'm sort of a "low brow" when it comes down
to it.

We cannot assume that the respondents interpreted the
terms of the question with real consistency, but they did at
least choose their places in what they could easily recognize
as a hierarchy of "intellectualness."

Table 2.5—Self-conception

(Per cent of those answering who checked)

"Intellectual"	15
"Educated"	56
"Serious"	26
"Low brow"	3
	100
N	1,795

In spite of their high educational levels, the bulk of the
respondents think of themselves as "educated people" and
only a minority consider themselves to be "intellectuals."
The same general conclusion holds, even when we take into
consideration education and sex, two variables which relate
to self-conception.

Table 2.6—Self-Conception by Sex and Education
(per cent Considering Themselves as "Intellectuals")

EDUCATION	MEN		WOMEN	
	Per Cent	N	Per Cent	N
No college	8	61	4	219
Part college	17	101	10	309
Bachelor's degree	13	136	8	263
Graduate work	28	362	19	293

On the whole, the proportion considering themselves as
intellectuals increases with education, and within each educational level is greater for men than for women. However,
even in the extreme group, men with graduate training, only
slightly more than one-quarter claim to be "intellectuals."
Further confirmation of these findings comes from our data

on "paths of life." We modified Charles Morris' value measurement scheme[3] and asked the respondents to rate four vignettes of values in terms of how much they liked or disliked them. The four can be labeled "Hedonism" ("Life is something to be enjoyed—sensuously enjoyed . . ."); "Groupyness" (A person should merge himself with a social group, enjoy cooperation and companionship . . ."); "Activity" ("A person must stress the need of constant activity—physical action, adventure, the realistic solution of specific problems . . ."); and "Contemplation" ("The contemplative life is the good life . . .").

Table 2.7—Marginal Distribution on "Paths of Life"

Path	"Dislike it quite a lot" or "Dislike it very much"	"Dislike it slightly," "Indifferent," or "Like it slightly"	"Like it quite a lot" or "Like it very much"	Total Per Cent	N
"Groupyness"	8%	45%	46%	99%	1,813
"Activity"	14	50	36	100	1,799
"Hedonism"	30	45	25	100	1,798
"Contemplation"	30	51	19	100	1,785

Except for "groupyness" the participants are not wild about any of the values, but it does appear that the values associated with extremes of "intellectualism," either toward the "Bohemian" pole of hedonism or the "mystic" pole of contemplation rank conspicuously low. Conversely, the modal American values of activity and group participation rank rather high, close to one-half of the participants endorsing "groupyness," and only 8 per cent rejecting it. While we have no general American norms for this measure, our distinct impression is that the Great Books participants do not depart conspicuously from basic middle class values, in which intellectual matters are certainly valued positively but do not form the core of the person's existence.

We have emphasized self-conception and values here, perhaps beyond their importance for the later analysis, but we would like to stress a point. Although there is some belief

3. Charles Morris, *Varieties of Human Value* (Chicago: University of Chicago Press, 1956).

that the Great Books program attracts "ivory tower" intellectuals and cult seekers, our evidence is essentially that the
participants, although highly educated in comparison with
the national population, on the whole share the general values and patterns of social participation of middle class
America.

If the point still needs clinching, we need only add that
when asked about specific magazines, 71 per cent reported
that they read the *Reader's Digest* regularly or occasionally,
and 65 per cent checked "Never heard of this one," for *The
Partisan Review*. However, when we note that we have no
national norms for "intellectualism," and we remember that
the question was worded in such a way as to discourage checking answers at the "high" end, we cannot say whether there
are more or fewer self-defined intellectuals in Great Books
than in other populations.

Sociologists usually think of age, sex, and marital status as
a cluster of variables which can be considered together as a
person's "life cycle role." By this, we mean only that, regardless of social status or region of residence or religion, single,
adolescent females have a lot in common; as do middle-aged,
married males.

Sixty-three per cent of the sample are women, 37 per cent,
men, a disproportion which is undoubtedly "significant" in
the sense that although in the general population there are
more women than men in the age ranges covered by Great
Books, the disproportion is not so great as in the program.[4]
Or, to put it another way, more women than men join Great
Books. We shall see, however, that among members, women
are much less active in the discussion and have lower "status"
in the groups, a finding whose implications will be important
throughout our analysis.

Three-quarters (74 per cent) of the women are married;

4. Our analysis of the sample suggests that there are relatively more men
in the small towns which are under-represented in our study. Even there,
though, women form a slight majority.

15 per cent are single; and 11 per cent are widowed or divorced. The bulk of the married women are "housewives" with no part-time job or studies; while almost all of the single women are employed full time; and most of the "ex-married" women are employed. Almost all the men work full time. There were very few "students" or "retired" in our sample. Of the men, 82 per cent are married, 14 per cent are single, and five per cent are widowed or divorced. The following table summarizes these data.

Table 2.8—"Life Cycle Role" Distribution of the Participants

Type	Description	Per Cent of Females	Per Cent of Males	Per Cent of Sample	N
1) Housewives	Married females reporting themselves as "housewives" with no job and not attending school	55	—	35	634
2) Working wives	Married females reporting full-time or part-time employment or full-time school attendance	19	—	12	214
3) Career women	Single women or ex-married women reporting full-time work	21	—	13	243
4) Other	Ex-married women reporting occupation as "housewife"	5	—	3	55
5) Husbands	Married males	—	82	30	556
6) Bachelors	Single males	—	14	5	93
7) Ex-married males	Males who are divorced or widowed	—	4	2	33
					1,828
Insufficient information to classify					81
		100	100	100	1,909

Table 2.8 is sort of a "collage" made up of sex, marital status, and occupation, in order to summarize the situation. We see that the bulk of the participants (65 per cent) consists of husbands and housewives; another 12 per cent of working wives; 13 per cent of "career" women; and the remaining 10 per cent of other categories. Putting it another way, we find 35 per cent housewives; 25 per cent working

wives and career women; 30 per cent husbands; and 10 per cent others.

Before we leave the question of marital status, let us see how many of the married people participate as couples and how many do not. Table 2.9 below summarizes these data.

Table 2.9—Husbands and Wives

	Spouse Member of Same Group and in Sample	Spouse Member of Same Group, but Not in Sample*	Spouse Not a Member of the Group
Married males	264	35	257
Married females	264	37	547

* NORC interviewers collected from each leader the names of regular members of the group who were not present when the schedule was administered. By matching names, an estimate of "spouse loss" was made.

For the married men, 54 per cent attend the group on a couple basis; for the married women, 36 per cent. The 264 "couples" thus make up 27 per cent of our entire sample. More married women attend without their husbands than married men without their wives. This discrepancy goes a long way toward explaining the sex ratio of the program. If enough of the "missing" husbands were brought into the program to give the same proportion of spouses attending for both sexes, the proportion of women would drop from the observed 63 per cent to 54 per cent. Thus, our guess would be that the sex disproportion in the program is partly a function of the differential joint attendance of the sexes.

As one would expect from the above findings, the participants are concentrated in the early middle age span. Table 2.10 gives the distribution for the entire sample.

Table 2.10—Age Distribution of the Sample

Age	Per Cent
Under 29	16
30-39	37
40-49	24
50-59	14
60-69	6
70+	2
	—
	99

This distribution, however, is somewhat biased as our sample is deliberately inflated in the advanced years of participation, and the longer time participants are somewhat older than the beginners. A better perspective may be gained by comparing the first year members with college alumni in terms of their age distribution in the 1950 United States Census.

Throughout this chapter we will compare Great Books participants with United States Census data for all persons 25 years of age or older who have completed one or more years of college. There are many good reasons why we should not do this (e.g., the participants did not all attend college; our sample is more highly urban than are college people as a whole, etc.), but we feel some comparison is helpful and this is probably the best yardstick to use, even if it is a rubbery one. Almost all of our sample, after all, have attended college, and college alumni are more urban than the general population; so if we are going to make any comparisons this seems like the best possibility. We trust that the reader will remember through this chapter that any conclusions from the comparison should be considered only as hypotheses for further testing. For purposes of simplicity, from here on, then, we shall follow the magnanimous example of college development offices and refer to those people with one or more years of college as "alumni" rather than having to say

Table 2.11—Age Distribution of First Year Great Books Participants and U.S. College Alumni (1950)

Age	Per Cent of U.S.* College Alumni	Per Cent of First Year Participants†
25-34	34	42
35-44	28	30
45-54	19	16
55-64	11	7
65+	8	4
	100	99 (N = 675)

* Statistical Abstract of the United States, 1950.
† Forty-three participants under 25 were excluded to make the data comparable to the Census tables.

"persons 25 years of age or older in 1950 who reported one or more years of college."

Great Books beginners, it appears, run a little younger than college alumni in general. Thus, both relatively and absolutely Great Books participants are concentrated in the early thirties, although the program does cover a span from the '20's to the '70's. The "significance" of this conclusion is somewhat difficult to determine, although it may be worth noting that it supports findings later in the analysis that the participants are "busy" people and are not in Great Books to fill in a participation "void." The fact that they are clustered moderately in the "busy" years of the life cycle is consistent with this general conclusion.

We are now in a position to ask whether Great Books tends to select people of a particular marital status. Since in the general population marital status is correlated with age, sex, and education, it will be necessary to control these variables as best we can. The following table contrasts the per cent married in Great Books with the per cent married among those of the United States population in 1950 who had completed one or more years of college.

Table 2.12—Age and Marital Status of First Year Great Books Participants and College Alumni

Age	Married Men			Married Women		
	U.S. ALUMNI	GREAT BOOKS		U.S. ALUMNAE	GREAT BOOKS	
		Per Cent	N		Per Cent	N
25-34	75%	78	231	78%	80	422
35-44	89	90	226	78	80	345
45-54	89	91	135	70	75	201
55-64	86	85	47	56	55	103
65+	72	73	41	30	37	52

The distributions are remarkably similar, and we may conclude that the proportion married among the participants does not differ in any important way from the proportion in the general population of "college people." In fact, since our sampling bias is toward an underestimate of the proportion married, the program in general probably recruits married people disproportionately.

Our general impression is that "demographically" Great Books participants do not differ in any striking way from the general population of college alumni. One would perhaps have hypothesized that the program might attract the retired, or the separated who are at loose ends socially, but this does not appear to be the case.

Since education is one of the best indexes of social status in our society, we shall not expect to find any terribly surprising trends when we examine the occupations of the participants. It is clear already that we are dealing with an essentially upper middle class population.

Table 2.13 gives us sets of percentages which will enable us to draw our conclusions. It is based on the standard census classification of occupations, but excludes farmers and farm workers, as we only drew three such cases in our sample.

Table 2.13—Occupations of Great Books Participants and Urban Alumni

OCCUPATION	MEN		WOMEN	
	Great Books	Alumni	Great Books	Alumnae
Professional	65%	39%	53%	53%
Managers	20	22	6	6
Sales	7	12	4	5
Clerical	3	9	35	27
Blue Collar*	5	18	2	9
	100%	100%	100%	100%
N	640		434	
Not Working	11		669	
No Answer	41		81	
	692		1184	

* Skilled Workers, operatives, household workers, service, and non-farm labor.

When we compare the working women (remembering that they are a minority of women participants) with the job classification of the female alumnae, we find that the occupational distributions are strikingly similar. Or, to put it conversely, the working alumnae of the U.S. turn up in Great Books about proportionally to the frequency of their jobs in their group. The program may have a little higher "floor" for women since there are a few less blue collar workers among the participants, but the slight excess of clerical workers balances it.

For the men, the situation is somewhat different. There is a heavy excess of male professionals in the program and deficits in all other occupational groups, only the managers coming near their fair share.

How can we explain this sex difference? For one thing, we have been comparing all Great Books members with U.S. alumni, although some participants have not been to college. Because 21 per cent of the women have not been to college, we are comparing them with a more educated group in the population. However, 9 per cent of the men are not alumni, and the 12 per cent difference between the sexes among participants is not strong enough to account for the discrepancy we observed. Perhaps there is an occupational selection factor among men, but not among women.

Another possible explanation is suggested by the sociological proposition that the status of a household is determined by the occupation of the husband, not the wife. It might be that Great Books members are highly selected in terms of social status when compared with alumni in general. If so, we would expect: a) male participants would have higher status jobs than male alumni, and b) female participants would not necessarily have higher status jobs than alumnae, but their husbands (who determine their status) would have better jobs than alumni.

We can test these ideas by tabulating the occupations of the husbands of the woman participants. We will divide them into two groups, those who participate in Great Books themselves and those who do not. If we find a difference between the non-participating husbands and male alumni, we have evidence supporting our hypothesis of status selection, for this would indicate that even though the women themselves do not have higher prestige jobs than alumnae, their husbands do, and hence, their status is probably higher. If, on the other hand, we find an occupational difference between participating and non-participating husbands, this would support the hypothesis that for men, but not women, there is an occupational selection factor.

Table 2.14 gives the necessary data.

Table 2.14—Occupations of Participating Husbands, Non-Participating Husbands, and Alumni

Occupation	Husbands Who Participate	Husbands Who Don't Participate	Alumni
Professional	67%	53%	39%
Managers	21	28	22
Sales	7	9	12
Clerical	1	3	9
Blue Collar	3	7	18
	99%	100%	100%
N	275	481	

The table seems to support both hypotheses. The non-participating husbands have higher prestige jobs than alumni, which supports the status hypothesis, but the participating husbands are more likely to be professionals and somewhat less likely to be managers, which supports the hypothesis of occupational selection among men. Thus, it would appear that Great Books members of both sexes are of higher status levels even than the average American college graduate. At the same time, among men, professionals, whose jobs in some ways are "more intellectual," may be more attracted to the program than are businessmen.

If we percentage Table 2.14 horizontally instead of vertically, we find some more clues about the missing husbands. Forty-five per cent of the professional husbands accompany their wives; 30 per cent of the manager husbands, and 32 per cent of the salesman husbands. This is consistent with our ideas about the relationships among sex, status, and occupational values in recruitment to Great Books. If women tend to be selected on status, but not occupation, it will follow that many eligible women have businessmen husbands, since both professionals and businessmen have high status. Because of the occupational difference among men, these businessmen husbands will be less likely to come. Conversely, the professional men attracted to the program will have wives of the appropriate status level who will be likely to attend. It should be noted that this is not the whole story, for men as a group still bring along a greater proportion of their spouses (54 per cent) than women married to professionals (45 per cent), although the gap is narrowed somewhat.

Occupational status always has a time dimension, and the question of where a person is now does not answer the question of where he came from. Status mobility is particularly relevant in any social analysis of a program like Great Books. In a society characterized by relatively frequent mobility as a consequence of a changing occupational structure (the proportion of professionals among employed workers has doubled since 1910), people frequently end up much higher on the social ladder than their starting place. Since Great Books has a heavy proportion of professionals, an occupational group characterized by relatively high upward mobility rates, we may expect to find a considerable number of people who have ascended the ladder. Since, in addition, it would seem that a program like Great Books would be useful for obtaining social and intellectual skills missed during the ascent, it would be interesting to know whether the program tends to attract mobile people in high numbers.

The standard way of assessing mobility is a comparison of the occupations of father and son or father and husband, a path strewn with pitfalls due to the instability of occupations at both ends of the time span and the difficulty of assessing the status of occupations. Since the Census does not report such data, the standard reference data come from the 1947

NORC national survey, known as the North-Hatt study.[5] The following table is adapted from that survey.

Table 2.15—Mobility (per cent whose fathers were skilled, semi-skilled, service, farm, or labor)

PRESENT OCCUPATION	U.S.*	GREAT BOOKS† MALES	N	GREAT BOOKS‡ WIVES	N
Professional	42	29	399	23	413
Managers	56	20	116	19	177
Sales	53	27	60	32	57

* Proportion reporting "blue collar or farm" occupation for father for all respondents reporting a given current occupation, regardless of sex.

† Proportion reporting "blue collar or farm" occupation for father among Great Books male participants reporting a given current occupation.

‡ Proportion reporting "blue collar or farm" occupation for father among Great Books married women reporting a given current occupation for their husbands.

The trend of the table is clear-cut. Great Books participants in high status occupations today are, if anything, *considerably less mobile* than the 1947 American cross section. Whether this is because the program attracts less mobile people, or whether their high level of education required fathers who were relatively comfortably fixed, it remains that the "self-made man" and woman are *relatively* rare in our sample, although we do have 286 respondents (ignoring the unmarried women whose current social position is difficult to measure) who have made the transition from farm or blue collar origins to the upper white collar regions.

In spite of the relative situation, *vis-a-vis* the national sample, we should go wrong if we decided that social mobility is not related to participation in Great Books. One out of five of our respondents checked "becoming more sure of myself when talking with people of higher educational background" as a reason for joining the program (although, of course, not necessarily the only one).

In summary: Great Books participants are selected from the upper echelons of the occupational structure, even when compared with American college alumni. Men, in particu-

5. *Opinion News*, September 1, 1947, pp. 3-13.

lar, tend disproportionately to be "professionals," [6] possibly because of intrinsic aspects of their jobs. Women tend to be disproportionately recruited from the upper white collar levels, possibly because of status considerations. In terms of occupational origins, the participants appear less mobile than the general population.

In addition to education, family role, and occupation, one's social location also consists of a complicated web of formal and informal memberships and allegiances which tie the person to the larger social world. We shall consider the participants' ties both because our data tend to refute certain impressions about the program and also because these variables (along with sex, marital status, and education) play a major role in our analysis of group processes and membership retention.

Among the myths about Great Books participants is the claim that they are ivory towerists who have little or no connections with their communities. We can here suggest that, at least in its extreme forms, the myth is incorrect. The following tables probably cover the subject in all the detail it deserves at this point.

Table 2.16—Attachment to the Community

PER CENT CHECKING EACH RESPONSE IN ANSWER TO THE QUESTION, "WHAT IS YOUR EMOTIONAL FEELING ABOUT YOUR COMMUNITY?"

Response	Per Cent
"I feel I'm a real member of the community."	57
"I do like the community, but I don't feel I'm really a part of it."	37
"I rather dislike the community, and I definitely do not feel I'm a part of it."	6
	100
N	1,852

6. We have talked about professions at length without mentioning any specific ones. Considering only the respondents' occupations, the following professions each contributed more than 25 respondents: engineers (123); teachers (102); lawyers (61); accountants (39); journalists (36); physicians (34); college teachers (31). These seven groups account for 66 per cent of the professionals; and along with business managers (129) and secretaries (91) account for 59 per cent of the total participants reporting an occupation.

Table 2.17—Number of Civic Organizations to Which Participants Belong*

Number of Civic Organizations	Per Cent
0	12
1	33
2	25
3 or more	29
	99
N	1,505
No answer	404
	1,909

* Excluding religious organizations related to a specific congregation, formal civic office, informal sociability groups, and adult education groups.

Table 2.18—Number of Evenings Per Month Spent in Informal Visiting and Entertaining

Number of Evenings	Per Cent
0	2
1-4	48
5-8	36
9 or more	14
	100
N	1,772
No Answer	137
	1,909

In brief, majorities of the respondents report that they feel they are real members of their communities; belong to two or more civic organizations (if we assume that all of the no answer respondents to this question belong to none, 43 per cent belong to two or more civic organizations) and get together informally more than once a week.

Since religious readings bulk large in the repertory of the program, it is of interest to note the religious preferences of the participants. Do the "Thomist" readings tend to attract Roman Catholics, or does Milton pull in extra Protestants?

Until recently we have had no reliable religious data on a national sample, but a press handout of the Census Bureau in February, 1958, does give the results of a December, 1957, national sample of 35,000 households. Since education is not controlled in the Census report, we had figures from a 1955 NORC national probability sample tabulated for the religious preferences of "alumni" only. The results are summarized in the following table.

Table 2.19—Religious Preference

Religion	U.S. Population 14 and Over, 1958	U.S. Alumni, 1955	Great Books Participants
Protestant	66%	72%	62%
Catholic	26	19	10
Jewish	3	4	15
Other	1	1	1
None	3	4	12
	99%	100%	100%
N		402	1,752
Uncodeable			22
No answer			135
			1,909

Certain trends do appear in the table. First, the number reporting "None" is higher in Great Books than among the alumni. Second, the proportion of Catholics is lower in Great Books than among the alumni, who are, in turn, lower than the general population. Third, the proportion of Jews is higher in Great Books than among alumni, who show about the same proportion of Jews as does the general population. Finally, in spite of all these trends, it should be noted that the bulk of Great Books participants, as of the other two sample populations, are Protestant.

Now, the reader will remember that there was a heavy concentration of Jews in the largest cities in our sample. Since our sample is biased toward large cities, we have probably overestimated the proportion of Jews in the program and a properly weighted sample would probably bring their proportion down to something more like that of the alumni. This argument, however, works both ways, for Roman Catholics are fairly concentrated in urban areas also. Our guess would be that any sample which eliminated the urban bias would cut the proportion of Roman Catholics too. Balancing all these hypothetical findings together, our inclination would be to advance the hypothesis that if one controls for educational level, the program as a whole may recruit a somewhat lower proportion of Catholics and a higher proportion of "nones," but that other differences in religious preference are probably minimal.

In the the following table, the party preferences of Great Books members are compared with those of the alumni group of the 1955 NORC study and the general United States adult population from the same NORC national sample.

Table 2.20—Party Preference

Preference	U.S. Population	Alumni	Great Books
Democratic	51%	36%	48%
Independent	20	26	10
Republican	29	37	41
	100%	99%	99%
N	2,235	388	1,811

The trends in the above table are far from clear-cut. The proportion of Republicans increases considerably as one moves from the general population to the alumni and slightly as one moves to Great Books. For the other two allegiances, the trend is not straight. Great Books has more Democrats than the alumni and about the same as the general population, while the program has fewer independents than either comparison sample. To begin with, the proportion of independents may well be a function of question wording in our study as contrasted to the other survey. If, then, we ignore the independents, we find, among the party-identified, more Democrats in Great Books than among the alumni. There are two reasons for this. First, again as we saw

in the introduction, our urban bias has probably overestimated the proportion of Democrats in the program as a
whole, for in the small towns we find that 52 per cent are
Republicans and only 23 per cent in the very large cities. On
the other hand, let us examine the relationship between party
preference and education. In the following table we see the
per cent Democratic by education, for those who reported
themselves as either Democrats or Republicans.

Table 2.21—Education and Party Preference of Great Books Participants

Education	Per Cent Democratic	N
Less than high school	52	40
High school	50	141
Post high school	48	100
Part college	43	408
Bachelor's degree	44	403
Some graduate work	46	266
Master's degree	53	193
Other graduate degree	55	92
Ph.D.	62	98

The relationship appears to be curvilinear. That is, the
proportion of Democrats declines steadily as one moves toward the middle of the educational scale from either extreme.
Now, compared to the general population Great Books has
fewer low educated people, but it has many more highly educated people. The Democrats it loses at the bottom, it may
regain at the top. Thus, even if a less biased sample raised
the proportion of Republicans we doubt that it would
put them into an overwhelming majority.

In short, the only hypothesis we would hazard is that a
compensating process may be at work. The high status level
of Great Books participants may raise the proportion of Republicans in comparison with the general population, or
even in comparison with alumni. At the same time the dis-
proportionate number of people with graduate training may
insure that a fair proportion of Democrats are attracted. The

net result of these two tendencies may be to keep a fairly equal balance between adherents of the two parties.

§ Motivations

Categories such as age, sex, education, religion, and membership in community organizations are important to the sociologist because they are indexes of different motivations and behaviors. Thus, it is probably fair to assume that Democrats are more interested in effecting social change than are Republicans; women have greater maternal motivation than men; and highly educated people are more intellectual than those who have not gone beyond high school. Thus, from our analyses of the kinds of people in Great Books we can make some guesses about their motivations. For instance, we would guess that seeking social polish is fairly rare as a motive, since our analysis of status and mobility suggests that they are a pretty smooth group already. The links in these chains of reasoning get quite complicated though it could be that since Great Books members are highly educated, only the most intellectual non-college people come into the program and there is no relationship between education and intellectual motivations. Therefore, we shall conclude our description of the participants with some direct evidence concerning their motivations.

What do they want from the program? Probably the most important aspect of this question is that we need to ask it. Unlike a course in business English, French cooking, or arc welding, the purposes of an adult program in liberal education are not explicit. Proponents of such programs believe strongly that they have purposes and consequences, but these can not be laid out in a neat outline.

Our approach was to ask the participants what they wanted from the program at the time they joined. On the second page of our questionnaire we listed 24 specific motivations based on our impressions from pilot studies and conferences with administrators in Great Books and the Fund for Adult Education. Table 2.22 gives the relative frequencies of the items. The table suggests considerable diversity in motivation.

Table 2.22—Reasons for Joining Great Books

PER CENT OF RESPONDENTS CHECKING EACH PURPOSE AS SOMETHING THEY "DEFINITELY HAD IN MIND AS A REASON FOR JOINING—REGARDLESS OF WHETHER OR NOT GREAT BOOKS MET THIS EXPECTATION"

Rank	Reason	Per Cent Checking (N = 1, 904)*
1	To learn what the greatest minds in history have to say about the basic issues of life	64
2	Reacquainting myself with a cultural background which had become rusty	44
3	Improving my ability to analyze and criticize arguments	42
4	Escaping the intellectual narrowness of my occupation	42
5	Talking with people who have more intellectual interests than my usual "social" friends	40
6	Improving my reading skills	32
7	Getting a chance to express ideas I had been thinking and reading about	30
8	Escaping the intellectual narrowness of being a housewife	30
9	Improving my taste in fiction and poetry	24
10	Making new friends	24
11	Gaining insight into myself and my personal problems	24
12	Escaping the intellectual narrowness of my community	23
13	Becoming more sure of myself when talking with people of higher intellectual background	21
14	Supplementing an unduly narrow or technical college training	21
15	Gaining a better intellectual background for my participation in community organizations and community affairs	19
16	Developing common interests with my spouse	18
17	Becoming a more effective participant in group discussions outside of Great Books	17
18	Meeting people who are quite different from me	16
19	Finding solutions to contemporary problems	15
20	Other (any specific "write in")	10
21	Improving my ability to carry out my job through the intellectual training of reading Great Books	10
22	Increasing my ability to carry out my job through improving my ability to participate in group discussions	8
23	Developing the ability to lead group discussions outside of Great Books	8
24	Gaining the equivalent of a college education	7

* It was assumed that the five respondents who left the page blank were "no answers" rather than totally lacking in motivation.

Only one item on the list was checked by a majority of the respondents and two thirds of the items were checked by 30 per cent or less. It may be that we managed to leave all of the really frequent motivations out of our list, but the fact that only 10 per cent volunteered an additional motive in a space left for that purpose suggests that this is not the explanation.

Although no single motive was checked by everyone, most participants checked several motives. Only 7 per cent checked a single item, half checked six or more, and one fifth checked nine or more. This suggests that we should consider complexes of motives, rather than discrete reasons, and this was what we did.

The statistical method we used is called "cluster analysis." [7] The procedure involves computing the intercorrelations of all possible pairs of items.

A high coefficient (one which gets near 1.00 in size) indicates that the two motives are closely related; people who check one tend disproprotionately to check the other. A "cluster" consists of a set of motives which has the following general properties: a) each motive within the set is highly related to each other, and b) each motive within the set has a lesser relationship with other clusters and with the remaining unclustered motives. The net effect is like a grape arbor, with bunches of motives which hang together, even though they are all on the same vine. By this rather cryptic analogy we mean to stress that our method does not assume that the clusters are "independent" of each other. Rather, even though the whole set has a general tendency for positive interrelationships, the relationships *within* clusters are higher than the relationships *between* clusters.

---

7. Cf. Robert C. Tryon, *Cluster Analysis* (Ann Arbor, Michigan: Edwards Bros., 1939). For the technical reader, we may note that we used "Q" measures of association rather than correlation coefficients in our analysis. Since the technique is essentially "non-parametric" in its logic, we feel no real need to apologize except that the use of non-parametric measures in factor analysis type research seems to be an affect-producing activity.

Analysis of the data indicated four clusters and seven "lone wolf" motives. Details are presented in the following table.

Table 2.23—Cluster Analysis—(average Q relationship with)

Cluster	Motive*	Cluster A	Cluster B	Cluster C	Cluster D
A	23—Lead outside	.66	.23	.20	−.05
	21—Job via reading	.60	.45	.33	.14
	22—Job via group	.75	.35	.35	.17
	17—Participant out	.64	.39	.40	.28
	3—Analyze	.56	.50	.33	.27
B	11—Insight	.39	.60	.32	.35
	15—Background	.46	.49	.35	.29
	1—Great minds	.24	.66	.21	.30
	19—Contemporary	.44	.66	.21	.30
C	6—Reading skill	.37	.24	.48	.11
	9—Taste	.27	.29	.52	.31
	13—Sure of self	.49	.36	.61	.33
	24—College education	.16	.21	.44	.29
D	12—Community, escape	.10	.24	.18	.43
	18—Diff. people	.21	.35	.31	.45
	5—Intell. people	.18	.27	.29	.54
None	2—Reacquaint	.10	.14	−.12	.22
	4—Escape occ.	.08	.18	.16	.31
	7—Express ideas	.35	.40	.20	.31
	8—Escape, house	−.18	.09	.17	.19
	10—Make friends	.20	.16	.28	.34
	14—Narrow college	.21	.20	.14	.15
	16—Spouse	.06	.02	.04	.12

* The number refers to the number of the motive, as ranked in Table 2.22.

Let us look at Table 2.23, first in terms of technical details, and then in terms of substance. Within each "box" in the table is the average relationship of each motive with the other members of its cluster. Now, if our analysis has succeeded, Table 2.23 should show two patterns. First, each motivation should show its highest relationships within its own cluster. This is true for each row in the table. Second, reading down the columns, there should be no relationships outside a given box which are higher than those within. Here we do find one exception. Motive 3 in Cluster *A* (Improving ability to analyze arguments) has a higher correlation with Cluster B than one of the B's . . . (15: Background for participation). However, it has a still higher relationship with its own cluster A and is not a real member of B. We can probably say that this motive tends to overlap both A and B. Motive 4 (Escaping the narrowness of my occupation) was a candidate for Cluster D, but it brought the within-cluster average down too much, so it was left out. With these two exceptions, the pattern is that required by the definition of a cluster.

What, then, do these clusters mean?

Cluster A—"Stepping Stone."—The tightest cluster is A, which is made up of the following:

23. Developing the ability to lead group discussions outside of Great Books.

21. Improving my ability to carry out my job through the intellectual training of reading Great Books.

22. Increasing my ability to carry out my job through improving my ability to participate in group discussions.

17. Becoming a more effective participant in group discussions outside of Great Books.

(We excluded Number 3 because of the evidence we found that it may be a fellow traveler in Cluster B.)

What these seem to have in common is a focus on the job and on group discussions outside of the program. Now, we should note that Number 4 (Escaping the intellectual narrowness of my occupation) and Number 10 (Making friends) have quite low relationships with this cluster, so the issue does not seem to be "job" or "groupyness" *per se*. Rather, it appears to us that what these four motives have in common is a focus on learning specific techniques in Great Books that can be used as a stepping stone for success in other areas. The focus is not intellectual ("Learning what the great minds have to say" has a low relationship with this group), but rather on specific skills and techniques, and—we hate to say it—gimmicks. Cluster A appears to be highly pragmatic. It is also relatively infrequent, containing only motives of rank 17 or lower.

Cluster B—"Content."—The four motives in Cluster *B* are:

1. To learn what the greatest minds in history have to say about the basic issues of life.

11. Gaining insight into myself and my personal problems.

15. Gaining a better intellectual background for my participation in community organizations and community affairs.

19. Finding solutions to contemporary problems.

We have called this cluster "Content" because it seems to focus on the content of the books, and excludes group participation as a means or end. It does involve areas outside the immediate program, like "Stepping Stone," but these are quite intellectual and abstract, definitely not gimmicks. One might think of the "Content" cluster as the official motivation for the program. In its general aspect, motive 1, it is the most common reason; and in its applied areas (self, community, and world) it includes less frequent motives, but not the rare ones which are included in "Stepping Stone."

Cluster C—"Self-Help."—Cluster C includes:

6. Improving my reading skills.

9. Improving my taste in fiction and poetry.

13. Becoming more sure of myself when talking with people of higher intellectual background.

24. Gaining the equivalent of a college education.

One needs little ingenuity to figure out what underlies Cluster *C*. It is what a consultant to the study calls "They laughed when I sat down at the piano, but were they surprised when I began to talk about Plato," and we have decided to call it "Self-Help." It requires little comment, except to say that it does not include group participation in any form, and its elements have a wide range of frequency, being roughly less frequent as the aims appear more ambitious.

Cluster D—"Cosmopolitanism."—Cluster *D* is made up of:

5. Talking with people who have more intellectual interests than my usual "social" friends.

12. Escaping the intellectual narrowness of my community.

18. Meeting people who are quite different from me.

As we have noted, a case could be made for the addition of Number 4 (Escaping the intellectual narrowness of my occupation) here, although we chose not to.

Cluster *D* is made up of pushes and pulls. The push apparently is feelings of boredom and narrowness in the social world of the participants, while the pull is the hope that in the program one can find people who are more alert and intellectual. The elements here are both "social," since meeting people seems to be the cure, and "intellectual," since the lack thereof, appears to be the cause. We felt that "Cosmopolitanism" came pretty close to expressing the theme. Like the "Content" cluster, it includes one high ranking motive and others that are less common.

The remaining lone-wolf motives seem straightforward, and require no further discussion.[8]

These, then, are the clusters of motives we find in our data: 1) "Stepping Stone"; 2) "Content"; 3) "Self-Help"; and 4) "Cosmopolitanism." If you squint a bit intellectually, each appears to have a reasonable psychological unity, and the statistical pattern of Table 2.23 is fairly respectable, at least from our experience with cluster analyses. We should, however, note two qualifications:

1) These are the clusters of the things we asked about. No doubt, if we had asked different questions, or even slightly different questions, we might have gotten different clusters.

2) The clusters are based on what people *say* motivated them, not necessarily on what *really* did. Our general impression throughout the survey was that almost all of the re-

8. An exception: It seems to us that *a priori*, "Escaping the intellectual narrowness of being a housewife" should belong in "Cosmopolitanism." It just doesn't, and we found no good way to explain this.

spondents tried very hard to tell us the truth, but the human animal has a vast capacity to kid himself and make himself appear in a good light. What *really* motivates these people is probably beyond the capacity of behavioral science research to measure, but we should also remember that for many purposes conscious and overt motives can be as important as those tucked away in the depths of the unconscious.

How frequent are these motivational clusters in our sample of participants? No clear answer seems possible. If we examine the frequency of the individual items in the clusters, we see a wide range of ranks in Table 2.22 with the exception of "Stepping Stone," which only includes items of rank 17 or below. Frequency seems related more to the specificity of the motive than to its content. Clusters *B*, *C*, and *D* each include specific motives which are among the first five in the rank order, and we suspect that if we had written a very general item in the style of Cluster *A*, it might have drawn a much higher number of responses.

The closest we can come to an estimate is to calculate for each cluster the number of persons who checked at least one of the motives in it.

Table 2.24—Per Cent of Respondents Checking for Each Cluster at Least One Motive

Cluster	Per Cent
B) Content	71
D) Cosmopolitanism	68
C) Self-Help	51
A) Stepping Stone	28
N	1,904

By this rough criterion, "Content" and "Cosmopolitanism" appear to be the modal motivations, more than two-thirds of the sample mentioning at least one of their constituent items. "Self-Help" splits the sample in half, and "Stepping Stone" is quite rare. Two implications seem important here. First, pragmatic, applied motivations are characteristic of only a minority. If we consider "Content" and "Cosmopolitanism" as more intellectual motives and "Self-Help" and "Stepping Stone" as more practical ones, we find that only five per cent of the sample report purely practical motives, while 32 per cent report purely intellectual motives, and 53 per cent report both. Second, we notice that social interaction in the discussion group is quite important as a motivation. While such a purely sociable motive as "making new friends" is reported by only a quarter of the sample, the Cosmopolitanism cluster, which implies the significance of group relationships, is a dominant motivation. We shall not be surprised then to find that aspects of the group itself play a large part in determining whether a member will continue in the program. The important question is *"what* aspects of the group?" Because it turns out that role structure is the key variable, we shall next describe the roles these people play in their discussion groups.

§ Summary

We have examined the characteristics of our sample in considerable detail for two reasons. First, because this is a rather unusual sample for a small groups study, we wanted to describe the participants so that the reader would have some ideas about the ways they differ both from the general American population and also from the myths and stereotypes of the program. Second, as we shall see, one of the major themes of our research is the frequency with which social categories outside of the groups themselves play an important role, both as group compositional effects and as individual characteristics, in affecting the course of these discussion groups. We have simultaneously described our sample and "set up" most of the major variables which will be used in our later analyses.

What are the participants like? They tend to be very highly educated, quite married, somewhat female, disproportionately professional men, and wives of upper middle class husbands. They are infrequently "intellectuals," under-mobile, possibly under-proportionally Catholic. They are sociable, joining, Republicans, and Democrats. They come to Great Books looking for intellectual stimulation and the social rewards of interaction with people of similar motivation.

Where participants can be compared with the national population of college alumni, they tend to accentuate those qualities (mostly associated with high levels of interest and intellectual sophistication) which, in turn, differentiate the alumni from the general population.

In short they are well educated, high status, socially active, youngish, adults seeking intellectual and inter-personal rewards in discussion groups.

3. The Roles within Great Books Groups

Sociologists love to make conceptual distinctions, and among their favorites is the distinction between people, statuses, and roles. Ralph Linton, the anthropologist, provided the standard definition.[1]

> . . . A status, as distinct from the individual who may occupy it, is simply a collection of rights and duties . . . A role represents the dynamic aspect of a status. The individual is socially assigned to a status and occupies it with relationship to other statuses. When he puts the rights and duties which constitute the status into effect, he is performing a role.

Interestingly, social scientists do not have a standard operational definition of roles. Rather, they tend to use the idea as an explanation of findings. Thus, instead of determining the actual rights and duties of men and women and whether they are put into effect, the social scientist typically finds a consistent difference in the behavior of the two sexes and

1. Ralph Linton, *The Study of Man* (New York: Appleton-Century-Crofts, 1936) pp. 113-114.

interprets this as "sex role differentiation." It is clear, at least, that the data on roles should concern what people do, rather than their opinions or fantasies. However, it is not clear that everything a person does regularly is a role. To be a mother is to have a role, but to be left-handed is probably not.

It seems to us that the key to role-ness lies in Talcott Parsons's concept, "mutual expectation," [2] although the idea is also implicit in Linton's formulation. Following Parsons, we assume that social behavior constitutes a role only if it is characterized by mutual expectations, that is, when others expect you will do a particular thing and you do too. Without this agreement, there are no roles, merely social pressures or aspiration levels.

In order to measure roles in Great Books discussion groups, we collected information on participation in the meetings for each respondent in terms of: a) self-ratings of role performance, b) designation by other members of the group. Our assumption was that if these two measures agreed, we were actually measuring social roles. In this chapter we will describe the roles we measured, assess the degree of role differentiation, and then attempt to find factors involved in the allocation of roles to various members.

§ Measurement

One section of our questionnaire dealt with aspects of the discussion process itself. The key question went as follows:

> In many informal discussion groups a division of labor develops, so that some participants tend to specialize in certain aspects of the discussion process. Please check each of the 'specialties' below in the appropriate column.

2. Talcott Parsons, *The Social System* (Glencoe, Ill.: The Free Press, 1951), pp. 36-39.

Five roles were described:

a) Pulling the threads of the discussion together and getting different viewpoints reconciled
b) Joking and kidding, finding the potentially humorous implications in the discussion
c) Providing 'fuel' for the discussion by introducing ideas and opinions for the rest of the group to discuss
d) Making tactful comments to heal any hurt feelings which might arise in the discussion
e) Clarification, getting the discussion to the point by getting terms defined and pointing out logical problems.

Each respondent was asked to characterize himself on these dimensions by checking answers to the question, "I tend to specialize in this aspect: More than the other members of my group, about as often as the other members, or less often than the other members." In addition, the respondents were instructed:

> The same specialties are repeated below. After each, jot down the names of any members of your group who tend to perform this role frequently.

On the questionnaire six lines were placed before each specialty. Since no number was specified, the participants were free to write as many or as few names as they considered appropriate.

Thus, the respondent was asked to do two things. First, he was to rate himself on each of the roles. Then he was asked to mention, by name, the other members of his group who frequently performed a given role in the discussion process.

The data represent the individual's self perception of his role enactment and his perception of which of his fellow group members are frequent performers of the various roles. Hence, the data give us self perception and intra-group ratings of role enactment rather than ratings by outside observers.

This method has the advantage and, as we shall see, the disadvantage of generating two types of profiles with regard to the types of roles played in the discussion group by each individual.

(1) *Subjective profile:* the respondent's self perception of his role enactment.

(2) *Objective profile:* the other group members' perceptions of ego's role enactment.

Within each profile a respondent may be classified as active or inactive with regard to playing each of the various roles. For the subjective profile, if a respondent has stated that he tends to perform a given role more frequently than the other members of his group, he is considered as "active."

For the objective profile, if a respondent is mentioned by two or more other members of his group on a given role, he is considered as "active" in performing that role. One mention did not appear to be a strong enough criterion, especially since 28 per cent of the sample were husband-wife couples in the same group. The one mention a given respondent receives may simply be loyalty in naming one's spouse rather than a designation of frequency of performing a given role. By the use of two or more mentions, we obtain a *social* definition of a certain role rather than just one individual's viewpoint. A potential problem may be as follows. Since the groups vary in size from five to twenty-three members, is the number of mentions a person receives simply a function of the number of members in his group? A person in a group of fourteen members has a higher chance probability of being mentioned by two or more alters—for there are thirteen persons who could potentially name him—than a person in a seven member group whose number of potential namers is only six. The question here is whether the employment of two or more mentions as the operational definition of active role enactment discriminates against members of smaller groups and favors larger groups. Were this the case, we would expect that a greater proportion of the members of larger groups than of smaller groups would be classified as active role players. Were this situation to exist, we would not know whether this higher proportion of active members was due to the fact that a greater proportion of members in the larger groups were active members or that this was simply an artifact of the criterion which is being employed. The criterion of two or more mentions generates roughly the same proportion of active members for each of the roles in large groups as in small groups as the following table shows.

Table 3.1—Per Cent Receiving Two or More Mentions by Size of Group Membership*

ROLE	SIZE OF GROUP MEMBERSHIP	
	Less Than Twelve Members	Twelve or More Members
Fuel	19%	20%
Clarification	17	15
Threads	18	14
Joking	11	11
Tact	8	7
N	(746)	(1163)

* The average group size is around eleven members.

Hence, we may conclude that our operational definition of two or more mentions, while not perfect, is independent of group size.

Since the respondents rated themselves and mentioned other members of their group on all five roles, these roles all represent types of roles perceived by the respondents to be present in the discussion process. However, the relative frequency of the performance of these roles varies as the following table shows.

The Fuel, Clarification, and Threads roles, which may be classified as the task roles, are more frequently performed while the role of Joker and Tact, the social emotional roles, are less frequent. This order is evident whether one employs the objective or the subjective criterion.

Table 3.2—Subjective and Objective Profiles
of the Five Roles

ROLE	SUBJECTIVE PROFILE Per Cent Rating Themselves as "More Often than Others"	OBJECTIVE PROFILE Per Cent Mentioned by Two or More Other Members of Their Group
Fuel	23	20
Clarification	21	15
Threads	10	15
Joking	16	11
Tact	5	7
N	(1699)*	(1909)

* Respondents who skipped all five subjective role questions are excluded.

The small differences in Table 3.2 are of some interest. It appears that people tend to overrate their wit and underrate their integrative function of pulling the threads of the discussion together (the rank order of the two roles is reversed in the two distributions). However, over-all, the frequencies agree with each other very well.

Given that the relative frequency of the roles is generally similar by both criteria, to what extent are the subjective and objective profiles similar for a given individual? If self perceptions are integrated with group expectations, as is required by our definition of roles, there should be a strong correlation between the objective and subjective ratings. The theoreticians' definitions actually require a perfect correlation of 1.00, for they think of roles as present or absent, rather than as a variable with a range of possible degrees of institutionalization. In empirical research, correlations of 1.00 just do not occur, but it is difficult to set a norm above which one can consider a role as institutionalized and below which one doubts the existence of a social structure. In addition, one would expect that the degree of institutionalization would vary with group conditions. Therefore, we shall hope that there is considerable agreement between the two profiles, but not demand that it be perfect.

The following table shows the relationship between the subjective and objective role measures; that is, the extent to which ego's self perception agrees with alters' perception of ego. Agreement is highest on the social emotional roles, Joker and Tact. The task roles, Threads, Clarification, and Fuel, have somewhat lower, but quite respectable, associations and are very similar among themselves.

Table 3.3—Association Between Subjective and Objective Role Measures

Role	Q
Joking	.73
Tact	.68
Threads	.54
Clarification	.52
Fuel	.51
Number of Cases	(1909)

The deviations from a perfect 1.00 association may be due to a number of things. Possibly since the term "more than the others" was used in the subjective question and the term "frequently perform" in the objective question, the respondents may have used somewhat differing criteria in answering these two questions. Certainly, some of the problem comes from measurement error, although we do not know whether our relationships have been inflated or deflated by that *deus ex machina*. Another possibility is that the relationships we see are sort of averages over a range of groups some of which may have highly institutionalized role systems and some of which may have little or no agreement. We can not answer this question without considering all of the variables which might affect institutionalization, but we can consider some of the possibilities.

The question which must be raised and can be answered is whether there is a relationship between the degree of association between the objective and subjective ratings and such factors as the age and/or size of the group. The age and size of the group may be factors in the accuracy of a person's self perception and the perception of ego's role by the others in his group. If a group has met over a greater length of time, the role structure may have become more organized and defined. If so, the subjective-objective associations would be higher in older groups. However, the variations between young and old groups appeared to be more random than patterned as the following table shows.

Table 3.4—Association Between Subjective and Objective Role Measures by Age of the Group

ROLE	AGE OF THE GROUP	
	Groups in First Year of Meetings Q	Groups in Second or Higher Year of Meetings Q
Joking	.67	.74
Tact	.78	.63
Threads	.61	.51
Clarification	.41	.55
Fuel	.51	.55
Number of Cases	(642)	(1267)

With regard to the size of the membership, two logical expectations are possible. First, in a smaller group everyone knows everyone else and probably knows what roles the other members play. On the other hand, possibly a certain size is necessary before a clear division of labor can develop in a group. The data, as seen from Table 3.5 do not confirm either of these expectations. Since groups vary both as to size and age, a classification of groups may be made: (a) small young groups, (b) small old groups, (c) large young groups, and (d) large old groups. Do one or more of these types of groups tend to generate a higher degree of agreement between subjectively and objectively perceived role enactment? While there is some variation by age and/or size of group, no simple or consistent pattern of variation emerges. Furthermore, in Table 3.6 there is no consistent rank order in the size of the coefficients for the five roles, no one of which is consistently higher or lower in level of agreement.

The negative finding on age is probably more interesting than the finding on size. New groups have neither higher nor lower agreement than old groups. This suggests that these

Table 3.5—Association Between Subjective and Objective Role Measures by Size of Group Membership

ROLE	SIZE OF GROUP	
	Less than Twelve Members	Twelve or More Members
Joking	.74	.72
Tact	.49	.78
Threads	.64	.49
Clarification	.49	.58
Fuel	.32	.62
Number of Cases	(746)	(1163)

Table 3.6—Association Between Subjective and Objective Role Measures by Age of the Group and Size of the Group Membership

ROLE	SIZE OF GROUP			
	LESS THAN TWELVE MEMBERS		TWELVE OR MORE MEMBERS	
	Age of Group		Age of Group	
	First Year	Second or Higher Year	First Year	Second or Higher Year
Joking	.51	.75	.70	.74
Tact	.58	.52	.88	.72
Threads	.64	.63	.58	.30
Clarification	.34	.52	.56	.58
Fuel	.15	.34	.63	.65
Number of Cases	(181)	(565)	(461)	(702)

roles show up fairly quickly (most of our first year groups had only met on three or four occasions at the time of our first questionnaire) and do not depend on a long series of meetings. By further implication, these negative findings suggest that sociologists can go too far in hypothesizing that roles *arise in* social interaction *in response to* particular conditions in a group. These and other findings of our study suggest that at least some are "instant" roles which require no kneading or leavening in face-to-face interaction.

In general, we find moderate to fairly strong agreement regardless of the role, the age of the group, or the size of the group. Can we call this evidence for institutionalization? The question amounts to asking how high is high, but we believe that our evidence supports the idea that these are roles by our definition. Our statistical justification would be that agreement between the two measures is generally higher than the relationship of either to most of the outside variables in the study. To draw a conclusion on substantive grounds we would need comparison data on other roles. Our guess would be that in comparison with such social relationships as "mother," "father," "teacher," or "boss" these roles are less clearly institutionalized, but rather more structured than personal traits such as "thrifty," "optimistic," or "sincere." Our hunch is that the degree of agreement we see is about what one would find for other roles such as "friend," "opinion leader," or "neighbor" where there is no legal or formal organizational definition of the relationship.

§ Role Differentiation

The formal analysis of role structures may be thought of as a series of questions about correlations. When we correlate ego's and alter's perceptions of role performance, as we just did, we are asking questions about role institutionalization. Another set of correlations arises when we correlate roles with each other. We can think of this as the question of role differentiation. If two roles are highly correlated, people who tend to play one, also tend to play the other. Thus, the roles of father and breadwinner are undifferentiated in the sense that the same people tend to play both. (One could also intercorrelate roles over time rather than over people and find that even though the same person tends to have two given roles, he plays them at different times and they are differentiated over time, but not people.) The roles of husband and wife are highly differentiated, and anyone pedantic enough to run the correlation would find an almost perfect negative relationship. Still other roles, such as girl and student might show a random relationship. Thus, the degree to which roles correlate with each other is a measure of the degree to which a system of roles played at one time is differentiated.

The fact that our question was worded in terms of "specializations" indicates that our original idea was that the roles we listed were highly differentiated. This is because we wrote the questions to reflect some ideas about role differentiation which have developed in laboratory research on small groups, in particular the work of Robert F. Bales and his associates.[3] Our version of these ideas is as follows.

We may think of the process of group discussion as involving two kinds of work. One of these is getting the task of the group done. In the discussion groups dealt with here this would be the intellectual discussion of the various books which are on the agenda for the evening. This is the task or instrumental dimension of the group process. The second aspect of the work is commonly referred to in the small group literature as the social-emotional or expressive dimension. This is not directly concerned with accomplishing the task of the group, but rather with how the members relate to each other, and to the group as a whole.

A further distinction on the task dimension is suggested by the fact that the discussion process is one of give and take. On the one side, someone must start the discussion, that is, assume the responsibility for initiating the discussion—"providing fuel for the discussion." But what is done must be reacted to, hence the second aspect of the task dimension may be to "answer" what has been thrown out for discussion. This part of the task is the complement of initiating the discussion, namely coordinating the discussion, i.e., "pulling the threads of the discussion together" and "clarification of the discussion."

Likewise in the expressive area, we may have on the one hand the harmonizer, someone who "makes tactful com-

3. Bales' writings on this subject are scattered over a number of papers and book chapters. Michael S. Olmsted has provided a summary in *The Small Group* (New York: Random House, 1959), pp. 117-132.

ments" and keeps peace in the group. On the other hand, there is the joker whom Bales and Slater[4] suggest may serve the function of expressing negative emotional reactions as the harmonizer expresses positive emotional reactions.

With these distinctions in mind, we can classify our five roles as follows:

A) Instrumental
   1) Initiating (Fuel)
   2) Coordinating
      a) Analysis (Clarify)
      b) Synthesis (Threads)
B) Expressive
   1) Positive (Tact)
   2) Negative (Joking)

If a division of labor between instrumental and expressive specialization occurs, we would expect that the roles classified as instrumental would be highly inter-related and likewise that the expressive roles would be highly inter-related, but that there would be a low association between instrumental and expressive roles. Similarly, if functions are differentiated within these two areas, correlations should be low within a cluster. Table 3.7 shows the findings.

Table 3.7—Inter-Relations of Roles (Yule's Q)

	Joking	Fuel	Clarify	Threads	Tact
Joking	-	.68	.45	.51	.16
Fuel	.68	-	.83	.84	.55
Clarify	.45	.83	-	.88	.60
Threads	.51	.84	.88	-	.72
Tact	.16	.55	.60	.72	-

In some ways the table supports our analysis, but in

4. Robert F. Bales and Philip E. Slater, "Role Differentiation in Small, Decision Making Groups," in Talcott Parsons and Robert F. Bales, *Family, Socialization, and Interaction Process* (Glencoe, Illinois: The Free Press, 1955). Cf. also, Philip E. Slater, "Role Differentiation in Small Groups," *American Sociological Review*, XX (1955), 300-310.

others it does not. We would draw the following inferences:

1) Because all of the associations in the table are positive, this is not a highly differentiated role system. Regardless of the roles in question, a person who plays one is likely to play another. This suggests, and we will return to this point again, that there is some general dimension of role activity *per se* in addition to qualitative differentiation.

2) The three task roles (in the center of the table, set off by dotted lines) hang together rather strongly, and have much stronger relationships with each other than with the expressive roles. However, the task roles do not show the internal differentiation we predicted, the range of associations being the narrow one of .83 to .88.

3) The two roles which we expected to belong in the expressive dimension are relatively differentiated from the task roles (their associations with the task roles are lower than the intra-cluster associations among the task roles), and joking and tact are differentiated (they are almost independent of each other). Although our ideas are supported by the relative size of the coefficients, the absolute sizes are not what we would have predicted. Both expressive roles have high degrees of association with the task roles, and our best indicator of whether some one plays an expressive role is whether he plays a task role or not. Similarly, we would have been much more pleased if the positive and negative aspects of this expressive dimension had been negatively related, rather than random. The problem lies in the large number of people who are named to no role at all (64 per cent of the sample) who fatten up the "minus-minus" cells of the contingency tables. If we compute our associations only among those who play some role, we do find slight positive associations within the task roles, and negative associations between joking and tact, which suggests that among those who play a role, the differentiation is much as we predicted, but there is also a general gradient of "activity," such that anyone who

plays one role has a better than average chance to play another.

Hence, from theory and the data, three dimensions in the discussion process may be designated:

(1) a task dimension (instrumental): operationally defined by active role enactment on one or more of the task roles of Fuel, Clarify and Threads.

(2) a harmonizer dimension (expressive): operationally defined by active role enactment on the harmonizer role of "making tactful comments."

(3) a joking dimension (expressive): operationally defined by active role enactment on the joker role.

Since a Great Books group is a functionally specific group with the purpose of discussing the various books on the agenda, the expectation would be that most of the role playing among the active participants would be on the task dimension and a smaller portion of the role playing would be allocated to the expressive dimension. The relative frequency of the performance of each of these dimensions is as follows:

Table 3.8—Relative Frequency of Qualitative Role Enactment Among Actives—(per cent performing the role of)

Type of Role Enactment	Per Cent*
Task	81
Joker	30
Harmonizer	20
Number of Cases	(669)

* Per cents exceed 100 per cent because roles are not mutually exclusive.

We find that four-fifths of the active participants are active on the task dimension, somewhat less than one-third on the joker dimension, and one-fifth perform the harmonizer role.

Summing up the results of our two correlational analyses, we may conclude that these roles are *relatively* institutionalized in Great Books groups, and *relatively* differentiated into task, positive expressive, and negative expressive roles. There is a third correlational problem which we will consider next: the correlation between types of people and roles. Who plays what roles in these groups, and as we shall soon see, even more important, who plays any role? In the next section of this chapter we shall consider the problem of role allocation.

§ Role Allocation

We can begin by asking the simple quantitative question, "What factors affect the probability that a person will play a role?" Then we can ask, "Among those who play a role, what factors affect the kinds of roles different people play?" We will treat both questions because our previous analysis suggested a general dimension of role playing as well as qualitative differentiation, and also because the next chapter was analyzed before this one, and it turns out that the difference between role quantity and role quality is extremely important in that analysis.

Our analysis is organized around two broad theories of roles. The "intrinsic" hypothesis is that roles are produced by the specific conditions of interaction in a group. Groups differ in their personnel, and if role systems develop to meet the problems of getting the work done with the people available, it would seem that group composition (as discussed in Chapter 1) should play a part in affecting roles. For example, in Great Books, spirited discussion of different viewpoints may be thought of as necessary to get the work done, and one would expect that ideological differences would make discussions more spirited. If so, one would predict that, say, Democrats would be more likely to perform roles in groups where they were in a distinct minority and they were, in a sense, needed more. The intrinsic hypothesis suggests that we will find a number of compositional effects. On the other hand, there is the "extrinsic" hypothesis, suggested by our negative finding on group age and institutionalization. The assumption here is that particular kinds of people have particular propensities to speak up or keep silent in the discussion and that whether there are active members in a group or not is essentially a function of whether it has managed to recruit potentially active people or not.

When we turn to the research literature, we can make a case for either position.

Bales and his co-workers have worked on rather similar problems with laboratory groups over a long period of time. A large and rich research literature has come out of these studies, parts of which suggest that role structures (although not measured in a fashion which makes strict comparison to our study possible) are affected by group composition.[5] On the other hand, Strodtbeck and his co-workers, in a continuing series of studies of juries, have reported a number of correlations between personal characteristics and variables much akin to our measure of activity.[6] In addition, we have our own data.

We shall not examine in detail each of the compositional effect analyses on activity. Rather, we will begin at the end, with a summary classification, and then look in some detail at two particular groups of variables.

Chart 3.1 summarizes our findings in the format first seen in Chart 1.2, Chapter 1. We shall not repeat the rationale for this classification, referring the browsing reader to Chapter 1, which amounts to a justification of the chart.

Both group composition and individual attributes seem to influence activity. The group level ones are new and have not been discussed before. Their mysterious labels "Problem One," "Outside Contacts," "Joining," "Change in Schools,"

5. E. F. Borgatta and R. F. Bales, "Interaction of Individuals in Reconstructed Groups," *Sociometry*, XVI (1953), 302-20.

6. F. L. Strodtbeck and R. D. Mann, "Sex Role Differentiation in Jury Deliberations," *Sociometry*, XIX (1956), 3-11, and F. L. Strodtbeck, R. M. James, and C. Hawkins, "Social Status in Jury Deliberations," *American Sociological Review*, XXII (1957), 713-19.

Chart 3.1—Summary of Relationships with Role Activity

INDIVIDUAL LEVEL EFFECT	INTERACTION	GROUP LEVEL EFFECT	
		No	Yes
No	Logically Impossible	**Type 0** Age	**Type II** Outside Contacts (High) Local Interest (High) Joining (High)
Yes	No	**Type I** Political Pref. (Democratic) Status (High) Self-Conception (High Brow) Liberal-Arts-Knowledge (High) Education (High) Sex (Male) Marital Status (Married)	**Type IIIA** **Type IIIB** Problem One Religion (?) (Effect)
Yes	Yes	Logically Impossible	**Type IVB** Change in Schools (?)

Notes: The word in parentheses indicates the more favorable attribute in terms of relationship with
high activity
(?) indicates that the classification by form is somewhat ambiguous.

and "Local Interest" will be interpreted in the following chapters which attempt to show that they are indexes of a causal chain which is one of the major factors in program retention.

One compositional effect warrants discussion here, if only because it is the only example in our study of a type III*B* relationship where the individual and group level effects are opposite in direction. The attribute in question is religion, and a puzzling sort of thing it is.

The dichotomy is between Protestants and non-Protestants, and *P* is the proportion of Protestants in the group. At first glance, this appears to be one of those reversals discussed in Chapter 1 (Type III*B*), in which activity increases with the proportion Protestant, but within groups at a given *P* level non-Protestants are more active. However, our statistical criterion casts severe doubt on the linearity of the relationship, and it falls into no neat non-linear form. We note a decrease in activity as *P* rises to the .30-.39 range, and then a general

Chart 3.2
Religious Preference and Discussion Activity*

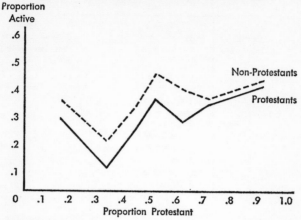

increase, but except for that we find difficulty in interpreting the measure. However, we note that for both classes of individuals activity is greater when P is above .5 than for any point below. Hence, in spirit, if not form, we can conclude that we have netted one of the strange $IIIB$ relationships. Why high proportions of Protestants increase activity, when Protestants tend to be less active themselves we shall leave as a problem for future research.

Having found that the group level effects fall into two classes, one which we don't understand at all, and another whose discussion we have postponed until the next chapter, let us turn to the individual characteristics which affect role activity. They appear familiar, if only because they are the personal characteristics which were analyzed in Chapter 2. By and large, the variables listed under Type I say simply that activity is a function of intellectual prowess and family role. The first is intuitively agreeable, and the second, when analysed in detail, has some interesting things to tell us about role structures in the larger society.

Therefore, the rest of this chapter will be devoted to a brief exploration of the inter-relations of the intellectual variables and a detailed analysis of family role as a correlate of discussion activity.

§ Intellectual Characteristics

Several of our measures (education, liberal arts knowledge, self-conception as an intellectual) suggest that one of the distinguishing characteristics of the active participant is his (and the word is chosen advisedly) greater degree of intellectual ability and interest.

Education is a good take-off point.

Table 3.9—Education and Activity

Education	Per Cent Active	N
No college	27	297
Part college	31	433
Bachelor's degree	37	414
Graduate study or degree	43	682

Table 3.9 simply says that the greater the formal education of a group member, the more likely he is to be named as an active participant.

Since education is strongly related to scores on our measure of knowledge of the liberal arts,[7] and both are related to activity, let us see what happens when we cross-tabulate education, knowledge, and activity. Knowledge scores are divided at the median, and education is dichotomized into those with bachelor's degrees or more versus non-college graduates.

Table 3.10—Education, Quiz Score, and Per Cent Active

KNOWLEDGE	BACHELOR'S DEGREE			
	Yes		No	
High	46%	(651)	43%	(264)
Low	34	(426)	22	(430)

7. This is a 32 item test, designed to test the participant's knowledge of history and literature. Because it does not play a key role in this book, we shall not describe it in detail.

Both apparently contribute. In each educational level, knowledge scores relate to activity, and in both levels of knowledge scores college graduates are higher than non-graduates. The pattern, however, suggests that the relationship is not just simple addition. Education makes more difference among low scorers than among high, and knowledge scores make more difference among the less educated than among the more highly educated. Put another way, the differences among those who are high on either education *or* knowledge are less than the differences between these three groups and those who are low on both.

Knowledge scores and education sort of measure the participant's intellectual preparation. Let us now see whether his intellectual stance, or self-conception, contributes toward activity when we control for these two variables. Self-conception is measured by answers to the question on intellectual self-conceptions described in Chapter 2.

Table 3.11—Self-Conception and Activity, Controlling for Education and Knowledge Scores (per cent active)

KNOWLEDGE	EDUCATION	SELF-CONCEPTION					
		Serious or Low Brow		Educated		Intellectual	
High	A.B.	43%	(54)	44%	(421)	54%	(160)
High	Less than A.B.	36	(106)	46	(102)	55	(44)
Low	A.B.	36	(59)	34	(310)	39	(38)
Low	Less than A.B.	21	(257)	23	(136)	25	(16)

The differences are not astounding, but within each row, activity tends to increase with intellectuality of self-conception, and within each column, activity increases with education and knowledge scores, although the educational difference in the high scoring group does vanish. The contribution of self-conception is particularly striking when one considers that we are holding constant not one, but two variables strongly related to activity and to self-conception, and also when we remember that activity is an objective rating, not a self-definition. People who think of themselves as intellectuals are more likely to be seen by others as playing an active role in the discussion, regardless of their formal education or liberal arts knowledge.

We can see our intellectual variables from another perspective when we compare them with another variable known to relate strongly to activity—formal group leadership role.[8] To begin with, leadership is strongly related to knowledge scores, although not strongly related to education when knowledge is held constant.

Table 3.12—Education, Knowledge, and Leadership (per cent who are group leaders)

KNOWLEDGE	BACHELOR'S DEGREE			
	Yes		No	
High	31%	(645)	26%	(263)
Low	15	(472)	11	(420)

Within each column there is a sharp difference in leadership chances by level of knowledge, but not much difference across rows by degree of formal training. Over-all, 24 per cent of the college graduates are leaders, as contrasted with 17 per cent of the non-graduates, but the difference is explained by their higher knowledge scores.

Let us now see the simultaneous effects of education, knowledge score, and formal leadership role on activity in the discussions.

Table 3.13—Leadership, Education, Knowledge Score, and Per Cent Active

Knowledge	Education	Leaders		Members	
High	A.B.	67%	(197)	36%	(448)
High	Less than A.B.	68	(68)	34	(195)
Low	A.B.	54	(63)	31	(359)
Low	Less than A.B.	38	(45)	19	(375)

8. We have analysed the informal roles in Great Books at some length without mentioning that the groups also have formally appointed leaders. These leaders are not paid and there are no particular requirements in terms of education or Great Books experience, but most of the groups in our survey have two members appointed as discussion leaders. As the following chapter, however, will explain, the program stresses a particular form of leadership such that the leaders do not lecture and are enjoined against expressing their opinions. Thus, they function more as "traffic cops" than as classroom teachers.

Leadership, as one would expect, is an extremely strong factor in activity. Regardless of the preparation level, leaders are much more likely to be named as actives. However, we also notice that among both leaders and members, there is a strong relationship between our preparation index and activity. Thus, the activity of members with high knowledge scores is almost equal to that of the least prepared leaders. Thus, we conclude that the relationship between preparation and activity cannot be explained by the fact that those members whose formal role in the group predisposes them toward activity have higher educations.

One should hardly be amazed to find that in a program devoted to intellectual discussion, those who are better prepared are more often named as active in the discussion. The finding is also in accordance with the results of Strodtbeck's research noted above.

One way of thinking of these results is to see them as another instance of a proposition from George Homans' theory of small group behavior:

> . . . the closer an individual . . . comes to realizing in all activities the norms of the group as a whole, the higher will be the social rank of the individual.[9]

If we accept the proposition as true, our findings suggest that, despite many opportunities for the Great Books discussions to turn into sociability groups, intellectual values have a high position in almost all groups, since it is those members who embody them who are designated as the leading contributors to the discussions.

Let us consider now two other social structural correlates of activity: political preference and social status. To begin with political preference, let us see its relationship with our two best predictors of activity—leadership and knowledge scores.

9. George C. Homans, *The Human Group* (New York: Harcourt, Brace and Company, 1950), p. 181.

Table 3.14—Political Preference, Leadership, and Knowledge Scores (per cent Democratic)

Knowledge Score	Leaders		Members	
High	54%	(258)	54%	(629)
Low	44	(107)	42	(744)

Political party is unrelated to leadership, but Democrats tend to have higher knowledge scores. Let us now see the relationship between party preference and activity, controlling for leadership and knowledge score.

Table 3.15 shows no consistent difference by party prefer-

Table 3.15—Party Preference and Activity, Controlling for Leadership and Knowledge Score (per cent active)

		PARTY PREFERENCE					
FORMAL ROLE	KNOWLEDGE	Democrat		Independent		Republican	
Leader	High	66%	(139)	81%	(26)	66%	(93)
Leader	Low	36	(47)	40	(10)	58	(50)
Member	High	41	(340)	34	(58)	30	(230)
Member	Low	27	(312)	24	(87)	21	(345)

ence. It may be that among members, Democrats are somewhat more active, regardless of their knowledge scores, but this does not hold among the leaders; hence, party preference is not a consistently important factor.

As for social status, Tables 3.16 and 3.17 tell a story similar to that of party preference.

Table 3.16—Status, Leadership, and Knowledge Score (per cent high status*)

Knowledge Score	Leaders		Members	
High	59%	(252)	58%	(610)
Low	44	(102)	50	(675)

* Status is measured by a coder's rating of the prestige of the occupation of the head of the household.

Table 3.16 tells us that high status people have higher knowledge scores, but that there is no consistent relationship between status and leadership. Table 3.17 indicates that when we hold constant knowledge score and leadership, we get a

Table 3.17—Status and Activity, Controlling for Leadership and Knowledge Scores (per cent active)

FORMAL ROLE	KNOWLEDGE	STATUS High		STATUS Low	
Leader	High	67%	(149)	68%	(103)
Leader	Low	58	(45)	42	(57)
Member	High	39	(353)	33	(257)
Member	Low	28	(337)	23	(338)

status difference in the last three rows, but not among high scoring leaders. Therefore, status is not a consistent contributor to activity.

In general, a good part of the relationships between party preference and status and activity can be explained through the finding that Democrats and high status members tend to have higher knowledge scores. These two social structural variables can not be considered consistent or striking factors in activity. Sex and marriage, however, cannot be disposed of so cavalierly, and require detailed consideration.

§ Family Roles and
Discussion Activity

While it is not surprising that intellectual characteristics should be related to activity in Great Books discussion groups, the fact that sex and marital status are important predictors is not so obvious.

Sex is always of interest, so we can begin with the relationship between sex and activity.

Table 3.18—Activity by Sex (per cent active members)

Sex	Per Cent	N
Male	53	694
Female	27	1187

Although a minority in the membership, the men are disproportionately more active participants than the women. One-half of the men are active in the discussion while only slightly more than one-fourth of the women are active. The individual characteristic of sex is a strong predictor of active participation.[10]

As for marital status, the expectation would be that the married are more active than the unmarried, for, generally in our culture, the married adult has a higher status than the unmarried adult.

Table 3.19—Activity by Marital Status
(per cent active members)

Marital Status	Per Cent	N
Married	40	1404
Unmarried*	23	424

* Includes single, separated, divorced, and widowed. Married is employed in the strict sense of married at the present time.

Married participants are more active than unmarried participants. Lest a combination of sex and marital status produce varying results, let us look at sex and marital status simultaneously with amount of participation.

Table 3.20—Activity by Sex and Marital Status
(per cent active members)

SEX	MARITAL STATUS			
	Married		Unmarried	
Male	57%	(555)	34%	(126)
Female	30	(849)	18	(298)

Sex and marital status appear to be independent predictors of activity in the discussion.

While sex and marital status contribute independently of each other, do they contribute independently of leadership and knowledge scores? To begin with, both are strongly related to our strong predictors.

10. This is in accordance with Strodtbeck's finding that men, in contrast with women, have higher participation in the jury task. Beck and Hawkins, *op. cit.*

Table 3.21—Sex, Quiz Score, and Leadership
(per cent male)

Knowledge Score	Leaders		Members	
High	56%	(266)	40%	(656)
Low	42	(111)	28	(759)

Table 3.22—Marital Status, Knowledge Score, and
Leadership (per cent married)

Knowledge Score	Leaders		Members	
High	86%	(261)	77%	(645)
Low	85	(110)	72	(734)

Table 3.21 indicates that males are both more likely to have high quiz scores and also to be leaders. Table 3.22 indicates that married members are more likely to be leaders, although their knowledge score advantage is small.

Now, let us see the effects of sex and marital status when we control for leadership and knowledge scores.

Tables 3.23 and 3.24 are clear and crisp. In each case, all

Table 3.23—Sex, Leadership, Knowledge Score, and
Activity (per cent active)

Formal Role	Knowledge	Males		Females	
Leader	High	73%	(148)	59%	(118)
Leader	Low	55	(47)	41	(64)
Member	High	49	(230)	27	(350)
Member	Low	41	(200)	19	(528)

Table 3.24—Marital Status, Leadership, Knowledge Score,
and Activity (per cent active)

Formal Role	Knowledge	Married		Not Married	
Leader	High	70%	(225)	50%	(36)
Leader	Low	51	(93)	29	(17)
Member	High	40	(499)	25	(146)
Member	Low	28	(532)	17	(202)

three variables show clear-cut relationships, a considerable sex and marital status difference appearing, even controlling for leadership and knowledge scores, with the leadership and knowledge differences holding within each family role category.

Taken together, these four variables provide a powerful predictor of individual differences in activity, since their contributions are cumulative. Table 3.25 shows activity as a simultaneous function of all four variables.

Table 3.25—Sex, Marital Status, Leadership, Knowledge Score, and Activity (per cent active)

FORMAL ROLE	KNOWLEDGE	MALE				FEMALE			
		Married		Not Married		Married		Not Married	
Leader	High	76%	(133)	46%	(13)	61%	(92)	52%	(23)
Leader	Low	56	(43)	—	(4)	46	(50)	23	(13)
Member	High	52	(205)	38	(55)	31	(294)	17	(91)
Member	Low	47	(158)	23	(52)	20	(374)	15	(150)

With the sole exception of the sex comparison among high scoring leaders who are not married, each of our four variables shows an effect in every comparison. That is, each of our four variables relates to activity, whatever combination of the remaining three is held constant.

The power of these four characteristics as predictors can be seen by constructing an index of activity-proneness on the basis of these variables. We can score each participant in terms of his total number of favorable characteristics (being a leader, having a high knowledge score, being married, or being a male), and look at the activity levels of members with different scores.

Table 3.26—Activity-Proneness Index (per cent active)

Score	Active	N
4	76%	133
3	55	354
2	38	583
1	20	530
0	15	150

Knowledge of these four variables goes a long way toward enabling us to predict the role performance of a Great Books member. Since, however, none of us is interested in actually doing so, Table 3.26 is of more interest to us in terms of its implications about roles. Our materials would seem to sup-

port both the intrinsic and extrinsic hypotheses, but when
the compositional effects are treated in detail in the next
chapter, we will see that they actually tend to corroborate
an extrinsic rather than an intrinsic interpretation. The role
of intellectual ability, although clear, is not surprising,
whether interpreted in a common sense fashion or in terms
of Homans' hypothesis. However, the strong contributions of
sex and marital status are of some general interest. They
suggest that to a large degree patterns of interaction developed in the larger societal social structure are carried over
into other social situations, and are one of the justifications
for our original claim that this study is one of comparative
social structure rather than small groups process *per se*. We
have now seen, and will see again and again in our analysis
the many ways in which the small group is affected by its relationships with the larger social structures in which it is
embedded.

The point is underlined when we turn to the question of
qualitative role differentiation. An analysis of correlates of
kind of role played among those who play roles suggests kinship roles are important here too, although we could find no
associations between role quality and education, status, political preference, intellectual self-conception, informal visiting,
and similar variables which, while playing a part in over-all
activity levels, do not relate to aspects of the task-expressive
distinction.

Again, let us begin with sex. In so far as boys and girls are
socialized in a differing manner, the expectation would be
that among the possible roles to be played in the discussion
group, those with a task emphasis would be selected by the
men and those with a social emotional emphasis by the
women. Qualitative type of role enactment may be looked at
from two viewpoints, total membership and active membership. Since the greater part of role playing is devoted to
the instrumental dimension, there is an association between
being active in the discussion and performing an instrumen-

tal role. Looking at the type of role enactment by sex based on the *total* membership, we find the following results.

Table 3.27—Qualitative Role Enactment among Total Membership by Sex (per cent performing the role of)

TYPE OF ROLE ENACTMENT	SEX	
	Male	Female
Task	44%	21%
Joker	18	7
Harmonizer	8	7
Number of Cases	(694)	(1187)

In this form, we could conclude that men overwhelmingly perform the instrumental role. However, considering that men are almost twice as likely to be active as women, we want to control for gross quantity of participation. Hence, to answer the questions about types of roles, we will employ the base of active members. This allows us crudely to hold constant gross quantity of participation and look at the more subtle differences in qualitative type of role enactment among active members.

As is shown in Table 3.28, 84 per cent of the active men

Table 3.28—Qualitative Role Enactment among Active Members by Sex (per cent performing the role of)

TYPE OF ROLE ENACTMENT	SEX	
	Male	Female
Task	84%	78%
Joker	35	25
Harmonizer	15	26
Number of Cases	(361)	(308)

are active on the task dimension, while only 78 per cent of the active women are active on this dimension. Hence, the direction is in accordance with the hypothesis; namely that men are more likely to play the instrumental role. However, a high proportion of the women play the instrumental role.

The high proportion of women who *are* task performers is to be expected for several reasons. The greatest amount of role playing is allocated to the instrumental task of getting the work of the group done. While the men are more likely to play the task role than the women, we would also expect that a good proportion of the women are active on the instrumental dimension, for the women are a majority of the membership, and getting the work of the group done probably demands performance of the task role by women as well as by men.

As for the expressive roles, the joker and the harmonizer, a contradiction appears here. Men are more likely than women to play the joker role, but women are more likely than men to play the harmonizer role.

The finding that men tend to perform the joker role more often than women is actually not surprising, for, to the extent to which aggression is part of expressiveness, we would expect the male sex role to be more apt to this kind of expressive facet. Our inclination is to suggest that since the adult male and the adult female must play both instrumental and expressive roles in society at large, though not to the same extent, the humorous facet of the expressive role is a man's way of playing a social-emotional role and the harmonizing facet of the expressive role is a woman's way.

It is of interest to note that in Table 3.7 "Joking" is fairly closely related to "Fuel" $(Q = .68)$ and "Tact" is rather closely related to "Threads" $(Q = .72)$. Because "Fuel" is a role involving starting interaction and "Threads" indicates reaction to someone else, it may be that men tend to play the aggressive form of both instrumental and social-emotional roles, while women tend to perform the more passive forms of these two types of roles. While our measure does not allow us to deal with this hypothesis on the instrumental dimension, we can look at the aggressive and the less aggressive forms of the social-emotional dimension.

Now, what about marital status and quality of role playing?

We have been interpreting our findings on sex differences in terms of a carry-over into the discussion group of habits and patterns of role performance. These habits and patterns are seen as a result of growing up in a society which defines the appropriate behavior of the two sexes in different ways. Similarly, we can look at marriage as a socially patterned system of role performances, instead of from the viewpoint of law or love.

Sociological theorists have maintained that, in the nuclear family, the male adult will play the role of the instrumental leader and the female adult will play the role of the expressive leader.[11] If so, we would expect that getting married would accentuate the sex differences we have seen, since the patterns of performance learned in one's new family will add to the differences originally learned in the parental family. However, this effect is probably different for the two sexes. For men, getting married probably doesn't affect the basic role system much, for the lives of adult middle-class men are heavily focused on their jobs (instrumental roles) before and after marriage. However, women typically work for a while before marriage, and hence shift from a heavily instrumental role situation to a much more expressive one when they take on the task of home making and child rearing. These considerations, taken together, give us the following predictions:

1) For men, marital status will show little relationship to role quality, but what difference there is will be for greater instrumental performance among married, as contrasted to single men.

2) For women, the married participants should show less instrumental and more expressive role performance when contrasted with single women.

Let us see what Table 3.29 tells us about our hypotheses.

Among the men we find no difference by marital status in task or joking, but, contrary to our hypothesis, more harmonizing among married than single men. Thus, it may be that

11. Talcott Parsons and Robert Freed Bales, *Family: Socialization and Interaction Process* (Glencoe, Illinois: The Free Press, 1955), p. 22, and Morris Zelditch, "Role Differentiation in the Nuclear Family: A Comparative Study," *op. cit.*, pp. 307-351.

Table 3.29—Qualitative Role Enactment among Active Members by Sex and Marital Status (per cent performing the role of)

TYPE OF ROLE ENACTMENT	MALE		FEMALE	
	Married	Unmarried	Married	Unmarried
Task	84%	83%	79%	78%
Joker	34	36	25	26
Harmonizer	17	5	28	19
Number of Cases	(319)	(42)	(254)	(54)

marriage, instead of adding to the sex differentiation for men, is associated with a somewhat more feminine role pattern.

Among the women, again, there is no difference in task and joking, but there is an increase in harmonizing for the married women.

Except in very small parts, we can hardly consider our hypotheses confirmed, the key problems being the increase in harmonizing for men, and the lack of any "de-instrumentalizing" among the women.

In short, Table 3.29 suggests that the effect of marriage upon role performance is to add to the expressive role performance of both sexes, while keeping a basic instrumental-expressive difference between them. Putting it another way, the effect of marriage upon role performance may not have anything to do with the sex differentiation of family roles. Rather, it may be that whether you are a man or a woman, having to live together and adjust to the presence of another person, adds to one's role performance in the social-emotional category of harmonizing, a role which is otherwise typically feminine.

To sum up our findings so far:

a) men tend to perform the instrumental and joker roles more often than women.

b) women tend to perform the harmonizer role more often than men.

c) married persons tend to perform the harmonizer role more often than unmarried persons.

We can see the effect of family role on discussion activity

in another light by comparing members who attend as couples with those who attend without their husbands or wives.

What might be the effects of attending group meetings with one's spouse rather than alone? All married persons have the common characteristic of membership in a family of procreation. However, for the married persons who attend the group without their spouses, their familial role would be latent since they are interacting in a non-family role situation where other members of their family are not present. During the meeting time of the discussion group, they are talking only to the other members, all of whom are non-family persons. The married persons who attend the group as couples, on the other hand, are talking not only to the other non-family persons in the group, but to each other. Since husband and wife are accustomed to a division of labor in role performance between themselves in the family, the carry-over of the role specialization in the nuclear family would be greater for those members who participate in the group as couples by virtue of the fact that the spouse is present and consequently the relational system of husband-wife interaction is stronger for them.

The underlying idea here is that kinship roles may be thought of both as categories and as relationships. Thus, to be a wife probably influences one's style of interaction, regardless of the alter in question, but it also prescribes a pattern of relationship with a particular person, one's husband.

The idea is interesting, but the analytical problems are tricky. The strategy we adopted was that of creating "artificial" couples and contrasting them with "real" couples.

The general procedure was this. In our sample of 1909 cases, we had 270 couples, and consequently 540 people who attend with their spouses. For each of these people we drew, using random numbers, another married member of their group of the opposite sex, to create an equivalent number of "artificial" couples. This means that for each of the 540 people who attend as couples, we can compare their discussion activity with their own spouses and also with another group of people who are in the same social category but are married to others.

Now, if the effect of marital status on role performance is solely that of learning roles associated with a new social category, we ought to get about the same results when we compare our 540 people with artificial mates, as when we compare them with their own. Conversely, if part of the effect of marriage is modification of role performance to adjust to a particular person, then we ought to get different results when we compare the 540 with artificial mates than when we compare them with their real mates.

We can begin with activity *per se* and then look at qualitative differentiation in type of role played.

To begin with, activity levels are essentially the same in the population of real and artificial couples. This follows from our probability mechanism for making up the artificial couples.

Table 3.30—Activity by Sex among Real and Artificial Couples (per cent active members)

SEX	TYPE OF COUPLE	
	Real	Artificial
Male	59%	58%
Female	29	30
Number of Couples	(270)	(463)

Now, however, let's pair husbands and wives and see what we get.

Table 3.31—Activity of the Wife among Real and Artificial Couples (per cent of wives who are active)

TYPE OF COUPLE	HUSBAND			
	Active		Inactive	
Real	44%	(158)	8%	(112)
Artificial	35	(266)	25	(197)

The differences in Table 3.31 are quite strong, and statistical tests indicate that they cannot be explained by chance fluctuations.

Let's begin with active husbands. We find for our married women that if their real husbands are active in the group, they have a slightly higher level of activity than when they are compared with artificial husbands. However, statistical tests suggest that this difference can be attributed to chance fluctuations. That is, having an active husband probably does not increase a wife's activity.

Now, let's look at the inactive husbands. A wife whose artificial husband is inactive is active in 25 per cent of the cases; but a wife whose real husband is inactive is active in only 8 per cent of the cases. This difference is significant at the .001 level.

These findings suggest that the effect of specific role relationships in marriage (as contrasted with the general role learning associated with entry into a given social category) is that the husband's activity level sets a ceiling on his wife's. If a husband is active, his wife's activity is not significantly higher but if a husband is inactive, his wife's level is significantly lower. More succinctly, these data suggest that one of the norms of marriage is that women do not talk more than their husbands.

When the same analysis is applied separately to the three qualitative types of role performance—task, joking, and harmonizing—what we find is that the relationship holds very strongly for task roles, moderately for joking, but in the case of harmonizing, inactive real husbands tend to raise their wives' activity slightly. The difference is not very strong, but it does suggest that our ceiling effect probably applies essentially in the types of talking that are associated with men. That is, we can revise our inference: One of the norms of marriage is that women never talk more than their husbands, in the areas of talking that tend to be the specialties of husbands.

The evidence here is all indirect. After all, we have not followed these respondents through their early socialization, nor observed the changes in interaction patterns which we assume follow from marriage. Nevertheless, from several points of view, the data here support the general idea that patterns of role performance are learned in the institutional matrix of the larger society, and to a large degree are transferred into new situations such as Great Books discussion.

§ Summary

Following the traditional distinction between people and roles, we have examined data on the role structures in our Great Books discussion groups. We grant that our findings may be an artifact of the specific roles we chose to include in our questionnaire, but in terms of these roles, we may conclude:

1) These roles are relatively institutionalized, in the sense that ego and alter tend to agree upon who plays what role.

2) This institutionalization is not affected by the age or size of the group.

3) These roles are relatively differentiated into task roles, positive expressive, and negative expressive types.

4) Along with the differentiation, there is a tendency for a person who plays any one of the roles to have a better than chance probability of playing any other.

5) Role allocation appears to be influenced by three sets of factors.

a) The proportion of group members who are named as active is affected by a set of compositional variables which will be analysed in detail in the following chapters.

b) The personal characteristics of intellectual ability and interest increase the probability that a person will be named as an active participant.

c) Kinship roles appear to affect activity level and quality of role through transferring into the small group, patterns of interaction learned in family situations. Both the categories of sex and marital status and also the relationship of husband and wife appear to affect role playing. Age is not related to role performance.

4. Drop-Out I:

Structure and Process
in the Discussion Groups

One year after the survey, NORC was able to determine the continuation status of 92 per cent of the individuals in our sample. We did not attempt to reach each participant, but rather we sent the leaders of the 172 sample groups lists of their members as of 1957. The leaders were asked to tell us whether the members were still in Great Books, and, if so, whether they were in the same discussion group.

The leaders were also asked to tell us why drop-outs had left the group. We found these data of limited value since it is our impression that the reasons given by the leaders and probably the reasons which departing members give their leaders are colored by rationalizations. There just can't be that many people who drop out of Great Books because they "are too busy." Hence, we shall focus almost entirely on relationships between data from the 1957 survey and from continuation status in 1958. At first glance, it would seem that without getting members' own reports we have made it difficult to assess the factors involved. We would not agree, for while we lack the insights we would gain from such data, we also avoid the error introduced by distorted perceptions and recollections. Thus, we have followed the informal maxim of survey research, that in order to find out why people do something one should not ask them "why" directly, but should rather find out what sorts of people do or do not do the something and then infer the "why" from the relationships discovered.

Table 4.1 summarizes the results of the follow up.

Table 4.1—Continuation Status of Individuals

	Per Cent	N
Continued in Same Group	64	1106
Transferred Groups	3	60
Dropped from Program	33	513
Presumably Dropped*		52
	———	
Total Per Cent	100	
Insufficient Information		154
Visitor†		24
		———
		1909

* "Presumably dropped" refers to cases where the leader's report was ambiguous, but the coders felt from the information available that the person was not attending the same group this year. They are treated as drop-outs in the analysis.

† 24 persons in the original sample were reported by the leaders at the time of follow-up as visitors, not members. In the original study they were treated as new members, since they *might* have gone on to become members of the group.

A little less than two thirds of our sample continued with the same group, one third left the program, and a small number switched groups. Since in this chapter we are looking at the materials from a group point of view, the transfers are treated as drop-outs. Their number is so small, however, that none of our conclusions would be changed if they had been treated as continuing. Thus, for all practical purposes, and the point is of some interest, to leave the discussion group is to leave the program.

In terms of groups, we find that about one third lost more than half of their members, including 17 per cent which succumbed; about one third lost between 30 per cent and 50 per cent of their original members; and a little less than one third kept more than 70 per cent of their members. We should note

Table 4.2—Per Cent Losses for Sample Groups

Per Cent of Group Continuing	Per Cent	Number of Groups
0 (Group Died)	17	27*
1-50	20	32
51-70	35	57
71-99	25	42
100	3	5
Total Per Cent	100	
No Information		9
		172

* This includes six groups which ceased to exist as independent entities by merging at least in part with other groups.

that these figures refer to members in the original sample. Since the groups gain as well as lose, the net effect is a different matter. When we consider gains and losses we find that 39 groups increased their size, 11 remained constant, 86 lost in absolute size, and 27 perished.[1]

Both in terms of individuals and in terms of the program, maintenance predominates over drop-out, but the margin is not such that drop-out can be ignored as an infrequent accident. Rather, it appears that drop-out and its converse, retention, are a function of certain factors which strengthen or loosen the member's ties to the program and to his discussion group. This chapter and the following two chapters describe these factors, using our statistical technique to isolate those which seem to work as a group level influence and those which operate at the level of individual factors. Although the complete argument is strung out over the three chapters, we shall try to show that most of the group level factors hang

1. A complete analysis of the factors in group survival should cover gains as well as losses. Thus, a group with a very high loss rate can survive if it also has a very high gain rate. Since we have little or no data on the characteristics of new members we have not been able to do such an analysis. What findings we do have suggest that in almost all cases, the variables we find associated with loss are *not* good predictors of gains. Thus, presumably, the group factors in recruitment of new members are of an entirely different type than those discussed in this report.

together in a fashion which suggests a causal chain involving social climates outside the groups, inter-personal relations outside the groups, participation in roles within the groups, and positive effects of participation in the program. In addition, for those variables which show important individual level effects, we shall look at multi-variate tables in order to assess their independent contributions.

We shall begin inside the discussion groups, analysing the effects of informal role systems and formal group leadership. Then in Chapter 5 we shall consider roles in family and community life outside of Great Books, and in Chapter 6 we shall look at some specific kinds of intellectual abilities and selected religious and ideological positions, as they affect retention.

§ The Discussion Process

The first—and we think the most important—set of variables involved in program retention consists of a number of characteristics related to the group discussion itself. They are group factors in two senses of the word. In the statistical sense, in terms of the technique described in Chapter 1, they show definite compositional effects. In the substantive sense, while each of them is tied to a specific person as an individual level attribute, we shall see that directly or indirectly they are involved in the actual process of group discussion. Thus, activity in the discussion, while a property of individuals, only comes to be because there are Great Books discussions in which one can be active.

We can begin with the two factors which, surprisingly enough, seem to have little importance from the group point of view. The first is size. While many sociological studies have shown that a group's size is correlated with its social structure and communication process, and many professional workers in the Great Books program have firm impressions about the optimum size of the discussion groups, our data show no simple relationship between size and retention.

Table 4.3—Age, Size, and Group Loss
(average per cent loss)

Size	First Yr.		Second-Third		Fourth or More		All Groups	
6-10	–%	(2)*	41%	(3)	42%	(11)	49%	(16)
11-15	61	(11)	54	(16)	27	(15)	46	(42)
16-20	67	(15)	41	(17)	47	(22)	51	(54)
21-24	47	(14)	30	(14)	40	(4)	38	(32)
25 or more	66	(7)	28	(7)	39	(5)	45	(19)

AGE OF GROUP

* The number in parentheses is the number of groups upon which the average loss was calculated

Table 4.3 shows no consistent pattern. Within the first year groups there is no trend at all; within the second and third year groups there is some tendency for larger groups to have higher average retention rates; and in the oldest goups there is no trend. This is not to say that there may not be some relationship between size and retention, but there is no simple pattern such that one can conclude that large groups or small groups are more successful.

When, however, we read the rows we find that in each case the first year groups have higher drop-out averages than the advanced year groups. This suggests that new groups, with less opportunity to develop a smoothly functioning pattern of discussion, may have a higher loss rate. Before we jump to this conclusion, let us apply the techniques developed in Chapter 1 to see whether new groups have trouble, or new individuals tend to drop out, or both.

In Chart 4.1, we see the data laid out in our standard format. *P* is the proportion of the group which is new to the program and can be thought of as a measure of the newness of the group as a group. We have three individual lines instead of two, but this does not change the general interpretation, the lines indicating the drop-out rates for people who

Chart 4.1
Exposure and Drop-Out

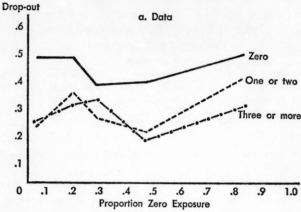

*N's for all compositional charts are given in Appendix.

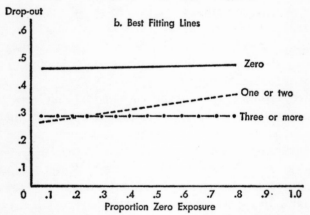

have completed zero, one and two, or three or more years in the program.

The individual difference is clear. Beginners have higher drop-out rates when contrasted with advanced members. There is no consistent individual level difference between the other two exposure groups. When we look at the directions of the three lines, despite some bulges here and there, no trend is visible. Statistical analysis indicates that there is no reason to reject the hypothesis that the data fit three straight lines parallel to the P axis; that is, by our criteria there is no group level effect of the age of the group, although beginners, as individuals, have high loss rates.

Age and size, it appears, are not terribly important for the survival of Great Books groups, except as both are related to the individual propensity for newcomers to have a greater loss rate. Presumably, the people who don't find Great Books to their liking discover this during the first year.

Let us now turn to a set of discussion variables which do show group effects. Only one of them is a direct measure of the discussion process, but since we will soon see that they are closely related to each other, we will consider all five in this chapter: outside contacts, activity, impact, effect on problem I, and change in schools.

We can begin with outside contacts. Each respondent was asked "How many members of your group (excluding your spouse) do you see regularly outside of the group discussions?" Individuals are divided into those who report one or more outside contacts versus those with none, giving us our attribute. The group variable is the proportion of the group with at least one outside contact, which we can think of as a rough index of the volume of the bonds between the members, aside from their program participation. Groups with low P values can be thought of as having few extra-program bonds, groups with high values probably have many.

In Chart 4.2 the A's are those with outside contacts, and P is the proportion of the group reporting one or more contacts.

The result is what we have called a type II relationship or pure compositional effect.[2] Within a given P level, there is no consistent difference between the retention of isolates and those with extra-group bonds; but for both types of people, retention varies directly with P. It would seem that a high

2. Unless otherwise specified, all zero order compositional effects discussed in the text are significant at or beyond the .05 level as described in Chapter 1. The significance of partials has not been tested.

Chart 4.2
Outside Contacts and Drop-Out

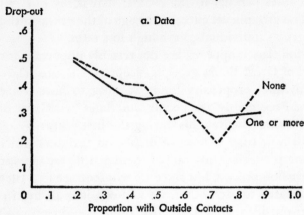

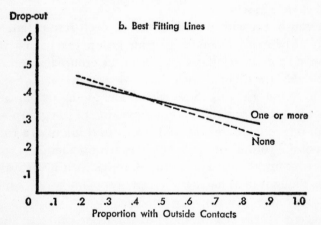

volume of extra-group interaction acts to create a favorable group situation. A number of speculations might be advanced to explain this finding, but we shall drop the matter for the moment. By the end of this chapter, however, we shall see that outside contacts may be interpreted as part of a complex chain of relationships which we shall call "the CAS" (for Content-Activity-Schools). By the end of Chapter 6 we will have a much more definite idea about how it works.

Since the previous chapter was devoted to a detailed description of the role structures of these discussion groups, it will probably not come as a great surprise when we report that role structures are important for program retention. Just as Chapter 3 considered role quality and role quantity, we shall consider both aspects as they relate to membership loss.

Sociologists today tend to interpret role structures (and almost anything else) from a "functional" point of view. While they try to avoid the Panglossian assumption that this is the best of all possible worlds and the teleological assumption that everything has a purpose, they still tend to assume that the important parts of a social system are important because of their consequences for the system, the most important consequence being the system's survival.

Bales, among others, advances a functional interpretation of role differentiation. He writes:

> A basic assumption here is that what we call the 'social structure' of groups can be understood primarily as a system of solutions to the functional problems of interaction which become institutionalized in order to reduce the tensions growing out of uncertainty and unpredictability of others.[3]

If role structures arise to meet functional needs, and if small groups have similar needs, then groups with different role structures might show differences in survival rates if one grants that loss of members is a reasonable index of inability to meet needs.

In order to test this idea, we can compare the drop-out rates in groups which do or do not have the specific role specialties discussed in Chapter 3. Because of problems in our case base, we cannot use all five of our roles in one table, but regardless of the combinations used, the net result is about the same as in Table 4.4. Because role quality is corre-

3. Robert F Bales, *Interaction Process Analysis* (Cambridge, Mass.: Addison-Wesley Press, 1950), pp. 15-16.

lated with role quantity (the more people with roles in a
group, the more kinds of roles there are), we shall control
quantity by grouping the cases according to the proportion
of members named to any one of the five roles. A plus in the
left hand column of the table means that a group has one or
more people named as playing a given role, while a minus
means that no one was named for that role.

Table 4.4—Group Level Role Differentiation, Role Volume, and Drop-Out (per cent dropping out)

(a) *Task Roles*

DIFFERENTIATION		PER CENT NAMED AS ACTIVE					
Fuel	Clarification and/or Threads	Less than 20		20-49		50 or More	
+	+	49	(102)	36	(616)	23	(514)
+	−	58	(89)	15	(20)	-	(0)
−	+	37	(79)	30	(56)	37	(16)
−	−	55	(232)	-	(6)	-	(0)

(b) *Socio-Emotional Roles*

DIFFERENTIATION		PER CENT NAMED AS ACTIVE					
Joking	Tact	Less than 20		20-49		50 or More	
+	+	67	(39)	35	(349)	24	(423)
+	−	48	(136)	28	(171)	25	(64)
−	+	69	(35)	16	(73)	13	(37)
−	−	49	(292)	58	(105)	-	(6)

The table shows no consistent column effects. The presence
or absence of the two socio-emotional roles, and the various
combinations of proactive and reactive task roles does not
seem to affect drop-out rates. While undoubtedly the roles
present in a group do have some functional consequences,
quality of role structure does not seem to affect survival in
terms of holding members.

However, in most of the rows, groups with greater proportions named as active members have better holding power regardless of the content of the roles. This suggests that role
quantity may be an important variable.

In order to see the quantity effect directly, let us examine
activity (defined as two or more group members playing a

Chart 4.3
Discussion Activity and Drop-Out

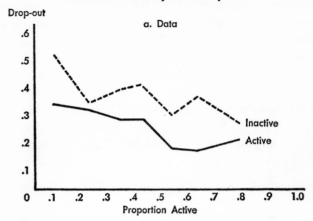

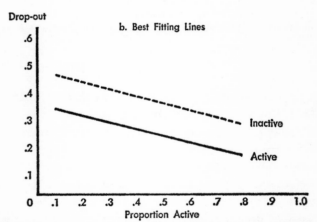

role in the discussions) in terms of compositional effect analysis.

Both relationships are linear by our tests, and the result is a clear type IIIA relationship, which shows a combination of individual and group effects. Within each P level, inactives have a much higher drop-out rate than actives, and within each class of individuals, drop-out decreases with the level of group activity. Both relationships are quite strong, and we note that the group effect is strong enough so that inactive members in groups with a high *P* value have a lower drop-out rate than active members in the least volatile groups. We may add activity level to our list of group effects.

The next three characteristics may be considered as a package, since they are all three measures of group output or effectiveness. The first is *"impact"* and is based upon answers to the following question.

> "On the whole, which of the following best describes your feeling about Great Books?"
>
> 1____ "It is a marvelous program and has had a genuine impact on me."
> 2____ "It is a fine thing and I enjoy it very much, but I can't say it has changed me much."
> 3____ "I have enjoyed some parts of it, but on the whole I haven't gotten much out of it."
> 4____ "I haven't gotten anything at all out of Great Books."

High Impact for individuals is defined as checking alternative 1 (checked by 42 per cent of the original sample); *low impact* is defined as any other response. Groups are characterized by the proportion of members reporting *high impact*. Chart 4.4 shows the relationship to drop-out.

The relationships in Chart 4.4 are non-linear by our statistical tests and don't fit any of our models clearly. However, we do note that among individuals, *low impact* people fairly consistently have a higher loss rate. Between groups, the pattern is less clear, but generally groups with *P* values below .5 have higher drop-out rates among both sub-classes of individuals. The pattern vaguely suggests what we have called a "step-function" such that above and below .5 there is little variation in drop-out, but a fairly sharp break occurs between groups with majorities and minorities reporting *high impact*.

The second effect characteristic carries the odd name of "Ef-

Chart 4.4
Impact and Drop-Out

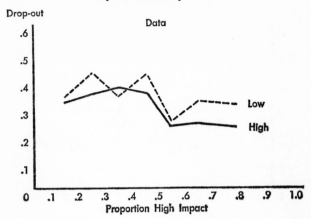

fect on Problem One" and is defined as follows. Each respondent was asked to list "the two or three most important problems facing your community today" and then to "indicate
below any ways in which you think your participation in
Great Books has affected your understanding of the problem
or your activity regarding the problem." Respondents are
coded simply as those reporting an effect and those not doing
so and groups are classified by the proportion reporting any
effect.

Chart 4.5 does not fit any of the logical models sketched out
in our introduction. Both lines are significantly non-linear,
but what they are is somewhat puzzling. In a general way,
with some clear exceptions, high proportions of no effect are
not a good omen for groups. As well as the consistent individual level advantage for the respondents reporting an effect,
we see a rough advantage for the groups with greater effectiveness over the groups with a lower proportion.

The third effect variable has another odd name, *"change
in acceptability of schools,"* which has nothing to do with
the respondent's education, but rather, with his answer to
the question, "Since you began Great Books have there been

Chart 4.5
Effect on Problem I and Drop-Out

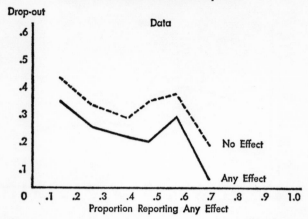

any particular authors or schools of thought which you once disliked, but now find more acceptable?" A member who said "yes" to the question is a changer, as contrasted with a non-changer who said "no," or didn't answer the question. Groups, in turn, are sorted by their proportion of changers, and when this is tabulated against drop-out we get Chart 4.6.

As we might expect from its two predecessors, change of schools is somewhat irregular according to our classification system. For the non-changers there is a linear decrease in drop-out as *P* increases. Thus, the more changers, the better the retention of non-changers. The line for changers is significantly non-linear without, however, taking any clear curvilinear form. When smoothed it suggests a rapid increase in drop-out as *P* rises to .6, and then a leveling off. The rise is so sharp, however, that around .6 changers have a higher loss rate than non-changers, although generally the advantage is with the former.

All three effect characteristics would belong in the discard pile, except that despite their idiosyncrasies, taken together, they suggest a common pattern. In general, for each of the effect variables, we find an individual level advantage for

Chart 4.6
Change in Acceptability of Schools and Drop-Out

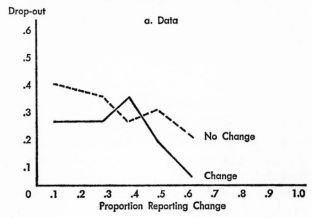

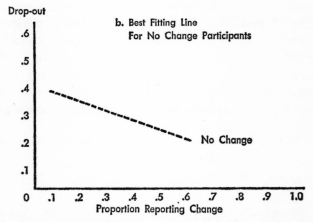

those who show the effect, and a tendency for high proportions of effect to raise retention among both classes. That is, in their joint implication, they suggest that some purer measures of "effect" might show a classical type III*A* relationship in which the individual effect radiates out to raise the success level among both types of individuals. We may hazard the hypothesis that success at the individual level breeds success at the group level in Great Books.

We can summarize the findings so far, with the following table.

Table 4.5—Discussion Process Effects

INDIVIDUAL EFFECT	GROUP LEVEL EFFECT	
	Yes	No
	Activity	Exposure
	Impact	
Yes	Problem One	
	Change in Schools	
No	Outside Contacts	

Table 4.5 summarizes, but it provides no insight into how these characteristics relate to each other nor whether they contribute independently to program retention.

We can begin our analysis by examining the group level inter-correlations of the five characteristics which seem to show a group effect. In Table 4.6 we see the Q coefficients (a measure of association for dichotomous relationships).[4] A high positive value of Q indicates that groups which are above the median on one proportion tend also to be above the median on the other; a Q near zero indicates no relationship; and a negative Q indicates that groups above the median on one proportion tend to be below the median on the other.

Table 4.6—Group Level Inter-Correlations of Discussion Process Characteristics

	Contacts	Activity	Problem One	Schools	Impact
Contacts	-	.42	.24	.12	.13
Activity	.42	-	.46	.37	.09
Problem One	.24	.46	-	.51	.27
Schools	.12	.37	.51	-	.48
Impact	.13	.09	.27	.48	-

The five form a distinct pattern such that each characteristic has a fairly high relationship with its neighbor and stead-

4. Calculation of a matrix of product-moment coefficients using deciles instead of above or below the median gives essentially the same results, although the values of the product-moment coefficients are much smaller, as is always the case. Those relationships with Q's of .27 and greater have r's significant at the .05 level or better.

ily declining relationships with other variables. Thus, outside contact relates fairly strongly to activity, relates moderately to effect on problem one, and has no very important relationship to the other effect characteristics. The pattern suggests, although it does not demonstrate, a causal chain which may be interpreted as follows: High outside contacts lead to high activity (which may be interpreted as vigorous discussions with many people participating). High activity (vigorous discussion) leads to seeing the relevance of Great Books for community problems (problem one). The perception of relevance, in turn, leads to changes in acceptability of various schools of thought. Finally, changes in acceptability lead to a feeling that Great Books has had a genuine impact. Schematically, we may put the idea as follows.

Outside Contacts → Vigorous Discussion → Relevance to Community → Change in Acceptability → Impact

Now, we may ask whether each of these factors contributes to program retention or whether only some parts of this chain are relevant. We don't have enough cases to consider all the combinations necessary for thorough analysis, but we can select three of our five variables. We chose outside contacts, activity, and change in schools, since they seem to summarize the model, which implies that a given type of social relationship influences the discussions which in turn lead to intellectual changes.

The groups were dichotomized on the three items on the basis of being above or below the median; all of the possible combinations were sorted out, and the per cent of drop-out was calculated for the resulting eight types of groups.

In Table 4.7, a + means above the median, — means below. Thus, the top row can be interpreted as follows. In groups which were above the median on proportion with outside contacts, proportion active, and proportion reporting change in schools, 26 per cent dropped out, this figure being based on 312 individuals in 30 groups.

Table 4.7—Group Typology and Drop-Out

GROUP TYPE				BASE N	
Contacts	Activity	Schools	Per Cent Dropping Out	Individuals	Groups
+	+	+	26	312	30
+	+	−	19	161	16
+	−	+	31	152	15
+	−	−	58	199	21
−	+	+	30	165	18
−	+	−	37	136	13
−	−	+	36	258	26
−	−	−	46	347	33

Let us now see whether active groups still show a greater retention rate when we control for outside contacts and change in schools, both of which are related to retention and to activity.

Table 4.8—Per Cent Dropping Out

TYPE OF GROUP			
Contacts	Schools	Active	Less Active
+	+	23%	30%
+	−	19	56
−	+	31	37
−	−	35	44

Controlling for each of the four possible combinations on contacts and schools, we find that groups above the median on activity have a better retention rate than groups below it. Thus, at the group level, activity contributes to program retention independent of contacts and our effect measure. That is, regardless of variation in the proportion of outside contacts and change in schools, groups which involve large proportions of their members in the discussion have better retention.

We can now apply the same test to our effect variable, change in schools.

Table 4.9—Per Cent Dropping Out

TYPE OF GROUP			
Contacts	Activity	High Change	Low Change
+	+	23%	19%
+	−	30	56
−	+	31	35
−	−	37	44

Except for the first row, there is a small tendency for high effect groups to have a more favorable retention rate, when we control for outside contacts and the activity level of the group.

Finally, let us look at outside contacts.

Table 4.10—Per Cent Dropping Out

		TYPE OF GROUP	
Activity	Effect	High Contacts	Low Contacts
+	+	23%	31%
+	−	19	35
−	+	30	37
−	−	56	44

In the first three rows of Table 4.10, we see a retention advantage for the groups with high volume of outside contacts, but in the bottom row, the minus-minus group, the difference reverses. That is, among groups which are low on both activity and effect, high outside contacts is an unfavorable sign. What we see is an interaction; i.e., in combination with activity and/or effects, outside contacts are a favorable sign, but in their absence high rates of outside social interaction are an obstacle to group maintenance. Thus, we can think of outside contact as a two-edged sword. When it leads, as it typically does, to active discussions and intellectual changes, it aids the group; but when it fails to produce these results it leads to a greater loss rate.

Before we reach a firm conclusion, we should check to see whether we still have a group level process here, or whether the pattern is spurious, due to the operation of the individual level effects we have seen. In order to do this, we need to show that individuals with the same personal characteristics have varying drop-out rates in our eight types of groups. In theory we should compare eight types of individuals (e.g., members with outside contacts who are active and have changed, members with outside contacts who are active and have not changed, etc.) in the eight types of groups. However, the case bases become so small that little reliable information comes from this. Therefore we shall treat the individual characteristics one at a time.

Table 4.11—Control for Individual Activity
(per cent dropping out)

	GROUP TYPE		INDIVIDUAL			
Contacts	Activity	Change	Active		Inactive	
+	+	—	17%	(97)	28%	(64)
+	+	+	19	(173)	34	(139)
+	—	+	10	(29)	36	(123)
—	+	+	29	(92)	32	(73)
—	+	—	25	(81)	55	(55)
—	—	+	25	(52)	39	(206)
—	—	—	32	(71)	49	(276)
+	—	—	45	(44)	61	(155)

In Table 4.11 the eight types of groups are arrayed according to their retention rate. The table gives us the drop-out percentages for active and inactive members. The progression is not perfect by any means, but there is a tendency for the order within a class of individuals to follow the group order. That is, regardless of the activity of the individual person, his probability of dropping out varies with the composition of his group. At the extreme we see twice as great a drop-out in the +—— group as in the ++— for both actives and inactives. Within each type of group there is a consistently strong individual difference between actives and inactives, but the group level effects also turn up, confirming our impression that activity works simultaneously as a group and individual factor in retention.

Table 4.12—Control for Individual Change in Schools
(per cent dropping out)

	GROUP TYPE		INDIVIDUAL			
Contacts	Activity	Change	Changer		Non-Changer	
+	+	—	14%	(21)	19%	(140)
+	+	+	26	(123)	25	(189)
+	—	+	27	(55)	33	(97)
—	+	+	26	(70)	34	(95)
—	+	—	24	(17)	39	(119)
—	—	+	30	(84)	40	(174)
—	—	—	38	(37)	46	(310)
+	—	—	45	(20)	59	(179)

Table 4.12 asks the same questions for individual differences in change in schools.

Table 4.12 is even more consistent than Table 4.11. In all but one comparison we see that non-changers have a higher drop-out rate. In addition, among non-changers there is a perfect rank-order correlation between the drop-out rates and the group types, and among changers the relationship only shows two negligible exceptions. In fact, in terms of percentage differences the variation in drop-out by group type is greater than the individual difference within a type of group.

Finally, let us consider contacts as an individual control.

Table 4.13—Control for Individual Differences in Contacts
(per cent dropping out)

	GROUP TYPE		INDIVIDUAL CONTACTS			
Contacts	Activity	Change	Yes		No	
+	+	−	19%	(129)	19%	(26)
+	+	+	25	(229)	20	(64)
+	−	+	27	(110)	42	(24)
−	+	+	28	(68)	33	(89)
−	+	−	33	(60)	36	(66)
−	−	+	35	(99)	38	(141)
−	−	−	41	(148)	46	(183)
+	−	−	59	(135)	44	(39)

Again, the same pattern appears. Within both sub-classes, drop-out rates increase as one moves from more favorable to less favorable group compositions. As we thought, individual level outside contacts are fairly unimportant, since no consistent differences turn up. However, we do see some support for our interpretation of the role of outside contacts. In the +−− group, it is those who have outside bonds who drop out at a greater rate, while those who do not have them have a lower proportion of losses. This is congruent with our hypothesis that when high bondedness does not lead to activity or effectiveness it has a negative effect on retention.

We are now in a position to summarize our analysis so far. Seven aspects of the group discussion were examined for individual and group relationships with program retention. Of the seven, five seemed to show a group effect. These five formed a pattern of inter-correlations which suggested a model of what might be going on. The model implies that close personal ties in a group lead to vigorous discussions, which in turn lead to a sequence of changes in the intellectual effect climate of the groups, which in turn lead to high impact. Next we turned to the question of the relationship between the stages in this hypothetical causal chain and program retention. Analysis of the data, simultaneously controlling for individual characteristics and multiple types of group characteristics, suggests the following.

1) High levels of group activity lead to high retention, independent of the group variables of outside contacts and change in schools, and also independent of the individual characteristics involved.

2) High levels of intellectual change lead to high retention, independent of the group variable of outside contacts, and to some extent independent of group activity (although in all cases the $++-$ groups do better than the $+++$), and also independent of the individual characteristics involved.

3) High levels of outside contacts lead to high retention rates only if they also lead to activity and change. If not, high levels of outside contacts are an unfavorable characteristic. This group effect occurs independent of the effect of individual characteristics.

We are now ready to suggest a modification of our model. The concepts in the model refer to group and not individual characteristics, and may be visualized as follows:

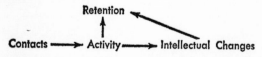

The diagram summarizes our interpretation, and shows contacts leading to activity and, in turn, to effects. In terms of relationships with retention, it shows activity and change leading to high retention, but outside contacts operating favorably only when combined with the other two effect variables.

Having outlined a scheme for looking at the major group level variables, as they affect program retention, let us now look at the individual level differences. We find that regardless of group composition, first year members, those inactive in discussions, and those who reported no program effects are more likely to drop out. Table 4.14 shows the simultaneous contribution of activity, exposure and impact.

Table 4.14—Exposure, Activity, Impact, and Drop-Out
(per cent dropping out)

GROUP TYPE		IMPACT			
Activity	Exposure	Yes		No	
Low	1st Year	47%	(139)	53%	(314)
Low	Advanced	47	(141)	30	(253)
High	1st Year	22	(40)	32	(110)
High	Advanced	13	(239)	21	(199)

Of the three characteristics, activity seems the most important. In each comparison in the table it produces a per cent difference of from nine to thirty-four points. Impact makes a difference in three out of four comparisons, but among inactive advanced participants, for some unknown reason, those who report a favorable effect are more likely to leave. Similarly, there is an exposure difference in three out of four comparisons, but among inactive, high impact members there is no exposure difference. Putting it a different way, high impact, advanced year members who are inactive in the discussions have a higher drop-out rate than one would predict from the over-all effects of these three variables.

§ Leadership and Discussion Techniques

The previous analysis may have seemed to imply that the prescription for success in Great Books discussion groups is:

"Find the correct compound of member characteristics, shake well, and apply bi-weekly." One wonders if this formulation leaves any place for leadership and specific techniques of discussion, or whether, once the mixture has been fixed, compositional effects proceed inexorably, regardless of the quality of leadership and style of discussion. Certainly, the idea that leadership and technique are unimportant is an unpalatable one, both because this is one area which is amenable to control, and also because a large volume of research in the social sciences suggests that leadership and styles of leadership are very important components in the group process.[5]

In order to explore this question, we shall consider in turn the following problems.

1) *Is there a relationship between leader training and program retention?*

The major efforts of the Great Books Foundation in maintaining the quality of the discussions lie in training programs for the volunteer discussion leaders (most groups have two leaders). Staff members of the foundation offer brief training courses for prospective leaders in a large number of communities. Although such training is not a requirement for leadership, most of the leaders in our sample have completed such a course. Therefore, it is of some practical importance to determine whether these efforts have a pay-off in more favorable retention rates among groups with trained leaders.

2) *Is retention affected by the members' preferences regarding techniques of discussion?*

Great Books discussions are supposed to proceed in ways specified by the Great Books Foundation, which provides statements of discussion techniques which it encourages or discourages. These techniques are believed to lead to more effective discussions. If this is true, it may be that groups

5. Cf., for example, Ronald Lippitt and Ralph K. White, "An Experimental Study of Leaderhip and Group Life," in Eleanor E. Maccoby, Theodore M. Newcomb, and Eugene Hartley, editors, *Readings in Social Psychology* (New York: Henry Holt and Company, 1958), pp. 496-511.

which accept these principles have more favorable retention experience.

3) *Is retention affected by the members' consensus regarding discussion techniques?*

It could be that even though the specific content of discussion techniques does not affect retention, the agreement within a group on patterns of discussion does. Thus, perhaps groups with nearly unanimous acceptance of a given approach do better regardless of the principle involved.

4) *Is retention affected by agreement between leaders and members regarding techniques of discussion?*

A second aspect of the consensus problem lies in agreement between leaders and members. Even though leaders constitute a small fraction of the participants in a group, their job, after all, is to lead, and it might be that agreement between leaders and members is the important type of consensus here.

§ Leader Training

While we have no direct measure of quality of leadership, we do know whether or not the leaders have completed the training course offered by the Great Books Program. Table 4.15 below shows the relationship of this variable to drop-out.

Table 4.15—Leader Training and Drop-Out

Leader Training	Per Cent of Members Dropping Out	Number of Members
All Trained	37	1024
One Trained, One Untrained	27	232
All Untrained	33	280
Leadership Rotates	32	103
No 1957 Information from Leaders	57	91

Two conclusions emerge from this table. First, that if the leaders are not interested enough to attend meetings (assuming that their absence on the evening we collected questionnaires was not an isolated instance), the chances for group survival are greatly reduced; and second, that leader training does not make much difference. The slight advantage that goes with being in a group with one trained and one untrained leader disappears when the level of discussion activity is controlled, as can be seen from Table 4.16.

Table 4.16—Leader Training, Activity Levels, and Drop-Out (per cent dropping out)

Leader Training	High Activity		Low Activity	
All Trained	26%	(370)	44%	(654)
Mixed	22	(173)	41	(59)
None Trained	20	(114)	42	(166)
Total	24	(657)	43	(879)

Apparently leader training does not have the simple relation to discussion quality that was hypothesized, since it is the mixed groups which have such high activity levels and therefore low drop-out. Whether the relationship between training and activity is accidental or causal is unknown, for we find the meaning of being in a mixed group to be somewhat obscure.

Does Table 4.16 then suggest that the leadership training program is of no value for Great Books? We doubt it, for there are a number of other considerations which enter into the picture. In the first place, leader training is not specifically designed to focus on retention, and it may be that trained leaders produce results in other areas than in retention. Secondly, we do not know anything about the differences between trained and untrained leaders. Thus, if persons who already have high skills in group leadership do not take the training courses, this would explain the lack of any difference.

§ Styles of Discussion

While Great Books has no party line in terms of attitudes toward the specific readings, the Great Books Foundation has a definite set of preferences regarding techniques of discussion.[6]

At first glance, the technique seems akin to "non-directive" group leadership, but upon closer examination it turns out that it is much more Aristotelian than Rogerian. As the leader training guide puts it:

> The function of a Great Books discussion leader can be reduced to this: getting participants to think and express themselves about great books. The leader performs this function in one way only, by asking questions.[7]

Along with the positive exhortation to question the members in order to enable them to analyze and evaluate the readings, Great Books leadership style includes a number of specific "don'ts." Leaders are warned not to give their own opinions:

> You will certainly have an opinion of your own, but beware! Revelations now, even outside the discussion meeting may be the beginning of your downfall.[8]

. . . not to introduce or sum up the discussion:

> . . . neither introducing a discussion nor summing it up is in order.[9]

. . . and not to provide historical or biographical background:

> We simply believe that, although the temporal and personal factors in a book will be illuminating to a scholar of that time or that person, those factors are not the distinguishing elements of that book's greatness.[10]

6. Cf. *A Guide for Leaders of Great Books Discussion Groups* (Chicago: The Great Books Foundation, Second edition, 1955).
7. *Ibid.,* p. 8.
8. *Ibid.,* p. 16.
9. *Ibid.,* p. 20.
10. *Ibid.,* pp. 21-22.

Unlike the non-directive group leader, the Great Books leader is encouraged to control specific aspects of the discussion. His major role is defined as "analytical questioning":

> The real mental discipline resulting from discussion, the real training in the liberal arts for the participants, depend upon the quality of the analytical questioning by the leaders. . . . It is always necessary to obtain clarification of meaning when the leaders themselves do not understand exactly what the person speaking means or when it is evident that others in the group do not.[11]

In addition, leaders are encouraged to keep an even balance among the members in order to prevent one or two from monopolizing the discussion:

> By the intonation of that new question you may even have to indicate gently that enough has been heard from one quarter, and others should have a chance.[12]

Of course, we have no data on how our groups actually carry out their discussions, but our questionnaire did include a set of items designed to measure the members' endorsement of the discussion techniques advocated by the national foundation.

Each respondent was asked whether the "ideal" Great Books leader should always, usually, sometimes, seldom, or never:

1) Tactfully squelch over-talkative participants.
2) Summarize the results of the discussion.
3) Give a short lecture on the historical and biographical background of the reading.
4) Refrain from communicating, even indirectly, his own opinion.
5) "Cross-examine" a participant to clarify the discussion.

11. *Ibid.*, pp. 30-31.
12. *Ibid.*, p. 24.

Members who accept the program's discussion style should agree with items 1, 4, and 5, and disagree with items 2 and 3. On the whole, the participants do accept these positions, but there is considerable variation. If we lump together "Always" and "Usually" for items 1, 4, and 5; and "Seldom" and "Never" for items 2 and 3, as acceptance of the program's techniques, and consider "Sometimes," as a neutral response, we get the following:

Table 4.17—Per Cent Accepting Various Techniques of Discussion

Item	Accept	Neutral	Reject	Total	N
Own opinions	59%	15%	26%	100%	1867
Background	57	22	21	100	1839
Squelch	55	38	7	100	1866
Summarize	43	23	34	100	1845
Cross-examine	42	43	15	100	1879

Slightly more than half of the members endorse the preferred position on giving opinions, background, and squelching over-talkative participants, but one can hardly infer a uniform acceptance of the techniques in the leader's manual.

Now let us look at the inter-relations of these items. Each was dichotomized as "Always" or "Usually" versus "Sometimes," "Seldom," and "Never," and Q coefficients were computed with the following results.

Table 4.18—Inter-Correlations of Technique Preferences (Q)

	Cross-Examine	Squelch	Summarize*	Background*	Own Opinion
Cross-examine	-	.20	.04	.13	—.02
Squelch	.20	-	.12	.04	.04
Summarize*	.04	.12	-	.66	.26
Background*	.13	.04	.66	-	.28
Own Opinion	—.02	.04	.26	.28	-

* Indicates that direction of the association was reversed so that "positive" always indicates agreement with the program's recommendations.

Now, if the program's advice was taken or rejected *in toto*, we would expect to find high association among the items; people who agreed with one would tend to agree with all of the others. Except for summary and background (the two items most distinctive of Great Books) no such pattern occurs. Therefore, we cannot hope to combine these measures into a single index of agreement with the program's position. We shall then treat each separately as a possible factor in retention.

We are now ready to tackle questions two and three on our list, by means of compositional analysis. If the answer to question 2 is "yes," that is, if there is a relationship between a member's position on these questions and program retention, we should find some sort of linear relationship, either at the group or individual level. If the answer to question 3 is "yes," we should expect to find some sort of parabolic group level relationship, with groups which are heterogeneous on these items showing different drop-out rates from groups which have high levels of agreement.

Chart 4.7
Ideal Leader: Squelch and Drop-Out

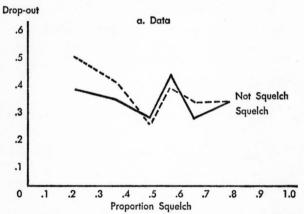

From Charts 4.7-11 it can be seen that none of the curves resemble very closely the typical parabola of the situation where consensus is important, nor do any of them fit any of our linear types, except summarize, which turns out to be a

Chart 4.8
Ideal Leader: Summarize and Drop-Out

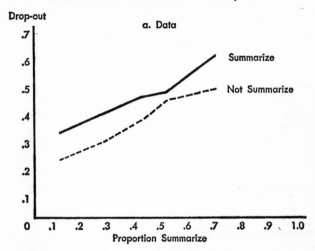

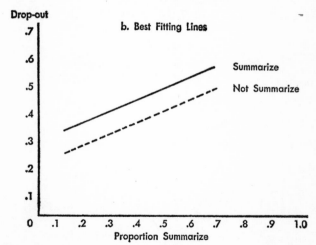

simple type III*A* relation, wherein the *A*'s are more likely to drop out than the *Ā*'s, and the higher the proportion of *A*'s, the higher the drop-out among both.

Since summarize does act like a compositional variable, it

Chart 4.9
Ideal Leader: Background and Drop-Out

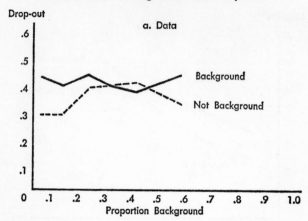

becomes important to see whether it fits in with the CAS model. The answer, as is so often the case, is both yes and no. As can be seen from Table 4.19, while it does relate to

Chart 4.10
Ideal Leader: Refrain and Drop-Out

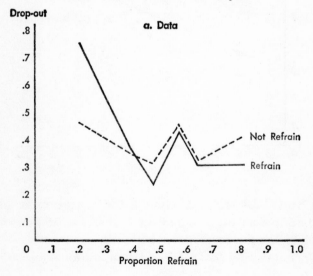

Chart 4.11
Ideal Leader: Cross-Examine and Drop-Out

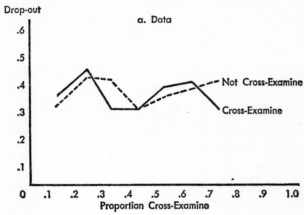

activity independent of contacts and schools, and to schools independent of activity and contacts, it does not relate to contacts at all.

Table 4.19—Per Cent of Groups above the Median on Summarize

Contacts	Schools	High Activity		Low Activity	
+	+	47%	(30)	60%	(15)
+	−	56	(16)	62	(21)
−	+	39	(18)	42	(26)
−	−	62	(13)	61	(33)
Contacts	**Activity**	**High Schools**		**Low Schools**	
+	+	47%	(30)	56%	(16)
+	−	60	(15)	62	(21)
−	+	39	(18)	62	(13)
−	−	42	(26)	61	(33)
Activity	**Schools**	**High Contacts**		**Low Contacts**	
+	+	47%	(30)	39%	(18)
+	−	56	(16)	62	(13)
−	+	60	(15)	42	(26)
−	−	62	(21)	61	(33)

Judging from its association with activity and schools, summarize would seem to be symptomatic of at least mild intellectual laziness, since groups high on it are likely to be low on activity and schools.

Given the relationship of summarize to activity and schools, and their relationship to drop-out, we next want to look at the partials. Table 4.20 gives us this information.

**Table 4.20—Summarize, Activity, Schools, and Drop-Out
(per cent dropping out)**

Activity	Schools	High Summarize		Low Summarize		Total	
+	+	28%	(227)	27%	(247)	27%	(474)
+	−	28	(160)	28	(137)	28	(297)
−	+	39	(207)	29	(202)	34	(409)
−	−	55	(347)	42	(200)	50	(547)

Within groups high on activity, the proportion endorsing summaries has no effect on retention, but among groups with fewer members in active roles, there is a difference, higher drop-out rates occurring in groups where many members want the leader to summarize. This suggests that summarization is involved in the CAS process described in the previous chapter. With this in mind, let us consider its relationship with some of our effect measures.

The previous chapter suggested (although our cross-sectional data cannot give us conclusive evidence on a dynamic process) that high volume of participation in discussion roles leads to intellectual changes and effects among Great Books participants, and that generally speaking, both activity levels and program effects contribute to high retention rates. Table 4.21 indicates that groups with high proportions in favor of summaries tend to be low effect groups, regardless of the specific measure in question.

**Table 4.21—Group Level Association Between
Summarize and Effects**

Variable	Q
Effect on Problem One	−.22
Change in Schools	−.28
Program Impact	−.37
Knowledge Scores	−.50

The more members who want summaries, the less likely it is that the group is high on program effects. Further analysis suggests that the relationship is not limited to one of these effects. Table 4.22 shows, for effect variables which are related to each other, that high summarize tends to be associated with each effect variable independently.

Table 4.22—Group Level Relationships between Summarize and Pairs of Related Effect Variables (per cent of groups high on summarize)

		Knowledge Scores +		−	
Schools	+	41%	(59)	57%	(30)
	−	42	(38)	76	(45)

		Impact +		−	
Schools	+	41%	(44)	51%	(45)
	−	43	(30)	70	(53)

		Problem 1 +		−	
Schools	+	40%	(48)	54%	(41)
	−	61	(23)	60	(60)

		Problem 1 +		−	
Impact	+	39%	(41)	45%	(33)
	−	57	(30)	63	(68)

Whether groups which want summaries are unlikely to show program effects or whether groups which show program effects are unlikely to want summaries, we do not know, but the relationships are strong enough to lead us to wonder whether summarize contributes independently to drop-out, or contributes only because it is related to low program effects. Table 4.23 provides the answer by showing the drop-out rates for participants in high and low summarize groups, when we control our four effect variables.

Of the fourteen possible comparisons in this table, only six show the original relationship between summarize and drop-out, and the rest are ties or reversals, so we feel safe in concluding that the original relationship is completely accounted for by the four effect variables, especially since the

Table 4.23—Summarize and Drop-Out, Controlling for Effect Variables (per cent of individuals dropping out)

Prob. 1	Schools	Impact	Knowledge	Low Summarize		High Summarize	
+	+	+	+	18%	(160)	14%	(42)
+	+	+	−	15	(26)	35	(54)
+	+	−	+	32	(63)	30	(91)
+	+	−	−	38	(24)	20	(15)
+	−	+	+	-	(0)	-	(0)
+	−	+	−	24	(41)	43	(44)
+	−	−	+	43	(47)	17	(6)
+	−	−	−	-	(0)	34	(67)
−	+	+	+	19	(32)	21	(34)
−	+	+	−	31	(16)	42	(60)
−	+	−	+	39	(83)	44	(78)
−	+	−	−	47	(49)	49	(73)
−	−	+	+	42	(59)	13	(31)
−	−	+	−	41	(66)	35	(34)
−	−	−	+	30	(89)	45	(117)
−	−	−	−	29	(35)	56	(194)

individual level effect of summarize is uncontrolled in Table 4.23. Substantively, then, we can speculate that summarize probably contributes to drop-out by preventing program effects.

Finally, we can turn to our fourth question. Although consensus on discussion techniques among the members does not seem to affect retention, we can put the consensus question another way. It may be that, since leaders probably do more to set the style of the discussion (after all, that is their job) than do members, agreement between leaders and members is an important factor. Thus, one might expect trouble where the leader wholeheartedly endorses the program's techniques, while the members reject them, regardless of the intrinsic merits of the techniques.

In Table 4.24 groups have been divided into "yes" and "no" on the basis of what the majority of participants in them say. Groups in which the leaders do not agree among themselves or did not answer have, for the sake of simplicity, been excluded from the analysis.

If leader-member agreement is important we should expect to find a difference between the drop-out rates in the two

Table 4.24—Leader-Member Agreement and Drop-Outs
(per cent dropping out)

LEADERS	GROUP				GROUP			
	Yes		No		Yes		No	
		Squelch				Summarize		
Yes	35%	(534)	31%	(255)	21%	(14)	- %	(0)
No	31	(145)	47	(232)	58	(131)	34	(1254)
		Background				Refrain		
Yes	- %	(9)	- %	(7)	36%	(711)	41%	(280)
No	40	(68)	35	(1391)	34	(64)	31	(81)
		Cross-examine						
Yes	32%	(296)	37%	(373)				
No	42	(19)	37	(509)				

types of diagonal cells. Specifically, if agreement facilitates retention, drop-out should be lower in the upper-left and lower-right cells than in the lower-left and upper-right cells.

Disagreement *per se* certainly cannot be said to produce drop-outs. In no case where there are sufficient numbers of respondents in all four cells do we find higher drop-out in the disagreement cells, and in the case of squelch, drop-out is lower in both disagreement cells.

There is, however, a pattern in Table 4.24 which may be worth noting. Except for "squelch," we seem to get higher drop-out fairly consistently in one, but not the other dis-agreement cell. That cell is always where the group is "yes" and the leader is "no." (We remember that the refrain item is worded negatively, and the high drop-out occurs in the cell where the group wants the leader to give opinions, but the leader is opposed to this.) From this point of view high drop-out may be caused by situations where the group wants the leaders to summarize, give opinions, provide background, or cross-examine, but where the leaders are reluctant to do so. This relationship, it should be noted, cuts across the recom-mendations of the program. Where the group seems to want what the program forbids, the leader's insistence on recom-mended techniques is possibly bad for retention, but when the group wants an approved technique such as cross-examination, and the leader is opposed, drop-out is also slightly higher.

The nub of the problem seems to lie in the fact that leaders (as one might expect) are much more orthodox than members. We can see this by looking at the case bases in Table 4.25 in terms of the number of members in the two types of discrepancy cells.

Table 4.25—Number of Members in Discrepancy Cells

TECHNIQUE	TYPE OF DISCREPANCY	
	Leaders Orthodox Members Heterodox	Leaders Heterodox Members Orthodox
Squelch	255	145
Summarize	131	0
Background	68	7
Refrain	280	64
Cross-examine	373	19

Regardless of the issue, it is much more likely that one will find a situation where leaders follow the book and members do not than vice versa. Thus, there are 131 members in groups where the leaders oppose summarize but the members want it, and no members in groups where the leaders want to summarize, but the members are opposed to this.

The summarize example was not chosen at random, for it not only shows the greatest skew between leaders and members (Table 4.17 indicated the highest rejection of the program's doctrine was on this item), but a careful examination of Table 4.24 suggests that our detailed analysis of the compositional effect of summarize may have been washed out. The deleterious effect of high proportions wanting summaries may well come from the fact that in these groups the odds are 90 to 10 that the leader will not want to summarize. Although the case base is ludicrously small (14 cases) we do note that where leaders and members both favor summaries drop-out is *lower* than in the modal case where both leaders and members follow approved doctrine.

Can we then draw any firm conclusions from our analysis?

Not many, for after all we have no firm evidence on what the leaders and groups actually do, and many a man's arm has been talked off by a person who would solemnly endorse non-directive techniques. However, the general line of our findings is: 1) that leader training *per se* shows no relationship with program retention, 2) that endorsement of the program's strategies of discussion techniques does not have an important effect except in the case of summarize, a conclusion about which there is considerable doubt after reviewing Table 4.24. All of these findings suggest that the specific content of the discussion style is not a major variable in group retention. However, it may be that in situations where either through overzealous application of the program's doctrine or because of personal inclination, the leaders do not provide a "service" desired by the group, high drop-out follows.

One can hardly offer this as an unqualified rule, but our data suggest that in terms of retention, the most effective leadership technique is "Give 'em what they want."

§ Summary

In this chapter we have applied our compositional analysis technique to the problem of membership loss in our sample of Great Books discussion groups, concentrating on variables which are intrinsic to the group discussion process. Our major findings are as follows.

1) Age and size of the groups have no compositional effects, but regardless of the proportion of experienced members, first year participants are more likely to drop out.

2) The *kinds* of roles played in the groups have no effect on drop-out, but role *quantity* is a strong group and individual level factor. The more members who are active in the discussions, the better the retention of active and inactive members. Within groups of a given level of activity, those

members who are named by others as playing an active role are more likely to stay with the program.

3) High proportions of members who see each other outside the meetings are associated with higher retention, but the relationship can be accounted for by the higher activity levels of groups high on outside contacts.

4) Generally speaking, high proportions reporting favorable effects of program participation are associated with higher retention. Within groups with similar proportions reporting a favorable effect, individuals who report such changes are more likely to stay.

5) Outside contacts, activity, and program effects are associated in such a way as to suggest a process (CAS) whereby social interaction outside the groups leads to high volumes of participation in the discussion, which, in turn, lead to favorable intellectual changes.

6) In terms of formally defined roles, leader training and acceptance or rejection of the discussion techniques recommended by the Great Books Foundation have no relationship with drop-out when one controls for CAS.

7) There is some evidence that in the cases where the members want the leaders to use a specific technique and the leaders do not, drop-out is higher.

We shall present a more complete interpretation of these findings when we have seen more of the evidence, but the findings reports so far seem to suggest the following conclusions:

a) Role performance in the discussions, regardless of the content of the roles, is the most important variable in retention, both at the group and at the individual level of analysis.

b) Role performance in the discussions is less affected by internal aspects of the group than by its relationships with the larger social structure.

5. Drop-Out II:

Family and Community Roles

While Chapter 2 attempted to persuade us that Great Books participants are far from a random sample of all the pigeon holes which make up American social structure, there is still considerable variation in age, sex, marital status, social class, and community involvement among our participants. We will now consider whether these indicators of roles played outside the group affect program retention. In particular, remembering how Chapter 3 suggested a carry-over from role performance in the larger society to role performance in the discussions, we shall ask not only whether these characteristics relate to drop-out, but also whether they appear to do so by affecting the CAS process. We should not be terribly surprised if they did, as both Chapters 3 and 4 suggested that to a large extent the role systems within the discussion groups are affected by extrinsic factors more than by internal ones.

§ Family Roles

We will begin with marital status, only to dismiss it. Chart 5.1 gives the drop-out rates for single and married members

Chart 5.1
Marital Status and Drop-Out

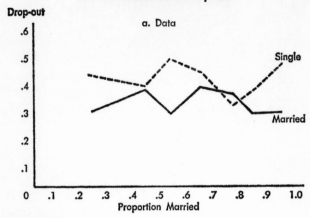

Drop-out

a. Data

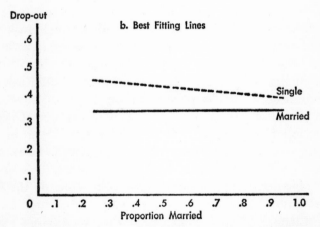

Drop-out

b. Best Fitting Lines

in groups varying in the proportion married. There is a tendency for single people to have higher drop-out rates, but for neither type of person do the rates vary with the marital composition. Marital status is thus a purely individual level characteristic.

Our second social structural characteristic is age and we are reporting on it out of a sense of dutifulness, not because we have any clear understanding of how (or whether) it

Chart 5.2
Age and Drop-Out

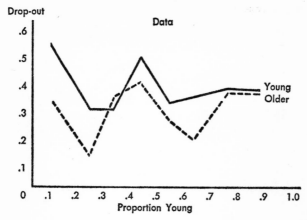

operates in group retention. In our survey, if not elsewhere, youth ends at age 35, and we have divided the respondents into those under 35 and those over that age. Groups are characterized by the proportion of their members who are "young," i.e., under 35.

At first glance, we see what appears to be a *W*-shaped curve for both age groups, with high drop-outs at the extremes and around .45. However, our statistical tests concluded that only the older group departs from linearity. Although it is possible that there is an intricate relationship between age composition and drop-out with optimal compositions around .25 and .60, our personal belief is that the picture is more congruent with erratic fluctuations than with some subtle process. However, we do note that in almost every instance, the younger people show higher drop-out rates than the older. Hence, we shall treat age as an individual characteristic and conclude that it has no meaningful relation with drop-out when considered as a group compositional variable.

Somewhat more definite findings, however, follow from the analysis of our other two social structural characteristics, sex

Chart 5.3
Sex and Drop-Out

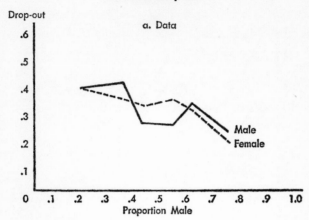

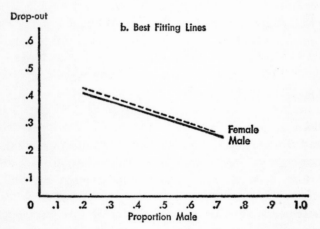

and socio-economic status. In Chart 5.3, we see the drop-out rates for men and women by the per cent male in the group. Our statistical check suggests that both relationships are linear and that there is no difference between the two lines. That is, we have a type II relationship in which drop-out decreases steadily with the proportion male, although there is no consistent sex difference in drop-out at specific *P* levels.

Although a number of explanations could be advanced to suggest why high proportions of women are associated with a high loss rate, we believe that the answer lies in the relationship between sex and the CAS process described above. We remember from Chapter 3 that men are much more likely to be active than are women. It is possible that our relationship is spurious, the high loss rates of the ultra-feminine group being explainable by their low activity rate. Since sex composition is unrelated to outside contacts or change in schools, we can test this hunch by examining the drop-out rates when groups are classified simultaneously by activity and sex composition.

Table 5.1—Activity, Sex, and Drop-Out (per cent dropping out)

PROPORTION ACTIVE	PROPORTION MALE 0-.29		.30-.49		.50 or More	
0-.19	51%	(200)	57%	(208)	39%	(94)
.20-.39	39	(150)	26	(172)	39	(132)
.40-.59	45	(119)	26	(257)	20	(114)
.60 or more	18	(93)	27	(106)	24	(85)
All groups	41	(562)	35	(743)	31	(425)

Reading across the rows in Table 5.1, we find that there is no consistent decrease in drop-out as the proportion male increases, within a given level of activity. Reading down the columns, however, despite some exceptions, we find that groups with a given sex composition show a negative relationship between activity level and drop-out. By and large, we conclude that sex affects group retention through affecting the activity level in the group. This does not mean that the sex difference is unreal. Rather, the analysis suggests the mechanism or process through which sex composition operates.

Because age and marital status appear to be individual level correlates of retention, it could be that the underlying factor is "life cycle role"; i.e., one line on the continuum from young adult to young married to oldster. Perhaps the losses are coming from the young married people whose family or career responsibilities compete with Great Books for time and motivation.

Although sex is not an independent contributor we have included it in Table 5.2 because it is an important aspect of life cycle roles. In addition, we shall control for activity in the discussions, the individual level variable which relates both to family roles and to drop-out.

Table 5.2—Age, Marital Status, Sex, Employment Among Married Women, Activity and Drop-Out
(per cent dropping out)

Activity	Age	MEN				WOMEN				
		Married		Single and Ex-Married		Married Not Employed		Employed		Single and Ex-Married
Low	Under 35	47%	(64)	55%	(44)	41%	(159)	42%	(55)	44%	(54)
	35 or Older	35	(133)	38	(26)	32	(206)	37	(69)	42	(138)
High	Under 35	26	(78)	28	(18)	21	(66)	27	(11)	12	(16)
	35 or Older	19	(204)	6	(17)	21	(104)	15	(39)	19	(32)

To begin with, in each comparison, activity, our key variable, shows a healthy effect. Age too holds up quite well, although not perfectly, two exceptions appearing among the active women. Because the age effect appears in both marital statuses in both sexes, and among working women and those not employed, we doubt that the mortality among the younger members can be attributed to the responsibilities of a young family. To what it can be attributed is something of a mystery. Inspection of reported reasons excludes spatial mobility as an hypothesis since we still get the age difference when we exclude members whose leaders reported that they had moved away. Interestingly, this is one of several examples where a variable which is favorable for recruitment—we remember from Chapter 2 that Great Books seems to recruit younger adults disproportionately—is not favorable for retention. Our marital status difference seems to have evaporated, however, the retention advantage of the married probably coming almost entirely from their higher levels of activity in the discussions. In short, so far, activity and age seem to be the individual level characteristics which hold up.

We can sum up the contribution of family roles to program retention as follows. In one way or another, age, sex, and marital status are related to drop-out. Youth, as an individual level attribute, is associated with drop-out for reasons which are not clear. Sex affects drop-out only through the influence of high proportions of women in lowering the activity levels of the groups. Married people tend to have better retention rates, but the difference disappears when one controls for activity, hence the effect probably comes from their higher activity level. The association between activity and marital status, however, does not appear so strong that the proportion married affects activity levels enough to make a difference in retention.

§ Social Status

Social Status or prestige is not actually a role in our society, but it is indicative of so many differences in role performance that it is worth considering here. Our measure is a prestige rating of the occupation of the head of the household. It should be noted that since a large proportion of the respondents are married women, the occupation in question is not always the respondent's. That such measures may still be important was suggested in Chapter 2 which showed the respondents highly selected in terms of occupational prestige. Respondents are characterized as "high" or "low" status on the basis of coders' ratings. The classification corresponds roughly to dividing the participants into those where the head of the household is a "free professional" or executive versus all others. We should stress that the "lows" are still

Chart 5.4
Socio-Economic Status and Drop-Out

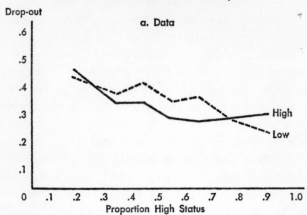

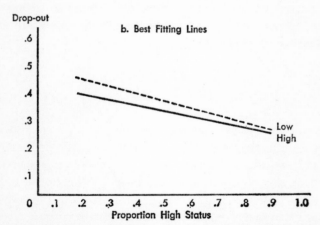

mostly middle class people, although typically "lower middle" rather than "upper middle." Chart 5.4 shows the group and individual relationships of status and drop-out.

The status relationship is on the borderline between our types II and III. As the per cent high status increases, drop-out decreases among both types of participants. There is also a slight tendency for low status persons to have higher drop-out rates for most *P* levels, but the difference is not terribly reliable according to our statistical criterion.

We can now ask whether, like sex, status composition affects drop-out through the CAS mechanism, or whether it is an independent contributor. To begin with, although status has no strong relationship with outside contacts or change in schools, controlling for the other elements in our model, there is some tendency for high status groups to be high on activity, as the analysis in Chapter 3 would predict on the basis of individual level relationships.

Table 5.3—*Status and Activity, Controlling for Outside Contacts and Change in Schools* (per cent of groups with .50 or more high status)

Contacts	Schools	Active		Less Active	
+	+	67%	(30)	53%	(15)
+	−	69	(16)	57	(21)
−	+	67	(18)	65	(26)
−	−	46	(13)	58	(33)

The differences are quite small, but in all but the — — comparison, we do find more high status groups in the high activity groups. In the — — group, however, we find a reversal. The reason for this will become clear in the next chapter when we consider education as a variable. For now, let us merely note the possibility that status is related to the CAS variables. Consequently, we shall want to examine the relationship between status and drop-out, controlling for CAS, and also for the individual level status in order to see whether status composition is an independent contributor to the drop-out process.

Table 5.4 meets this prescription, by indicating the proportion of drop-outs for high and low status individuals in groups which vary in status composition and also CAS composition.

The case bases become very small and unreliable in tables

Table 5.4—Status Composition, Individual Status, CAS Composition, and Drop-Out (per cent dropping out)

P, HIGH STATUS			HIGH STATUS				LOWER STATUS			
Contacts	Activity	Schools	.50+		0-.49		.50+		0-.49	
+	+	—	13%	(95)	25%	(4)	27%	(33)	29%	(17)
+	+	+	25	(110)	29	(35)	24	(58)	26	(74)
+	—	+	41	(39)	*29	(24)	12	(17)	33	(51)
—	+	+	19	(57)	42	(24)	27	(33)	41	(39)
—	+	—	39	(38)	*22	(23)	32	(19)	38	(48)
—	—	+	32	(85)	46	(26)	37	(43)	42	(59)
—	—	—	39	(140)	50	(36)	49	(63)	52	(75)
+	—	—	41	(51)	48	(27)	49	(35)	68	(63)

like Table 5.4, so we have to draw our conclusions from the overall pattern. We note that there are 16 comparisons which contrast status compositions, holding constant individual status and CAS. Since in 14 out of the 16 (the two exceptions are marked with an asterisk) the drop-out rates are lower in the groups which have more high status people, we may conclude that status composition is a pretty consistent group level contributor to program retention. Status as an individual attribute is favorable in only ten out of sixteen comparisons. Thus, although status is an important personal characteristic for recruitment, it plays little independent role in program retention.

We should now reverse the question and ask whether, when status composition is controlled, the CAS characteristics still show a relationship with drop-out. They do. Of the 16 comparisons involving activity, drop-out was lower in the high activity groups in 13 cases, higher in two, and tied in one. Change in schools shows 11 comparisons in the predicted direction, two ties, and three reversals. Contacts, which we have already seen is not a consistent performer, has a slightly lower record, 10 comparisons in the predicted direction, one tie, and five reversals. However, since we note that two of the reversals and the tie are in the +—— type, these results are consistent with our previous interpretation of the effect of this characteristic.

§ Outside Interaction

If there is any point which we hope we have made so far, it is that interaction outside the discussion groups has a strong relationship with interaction within the groups and consequently on their retention rates. We have considered outside contacts, the degree to which group members see each other aside from the regular Great Books sessions. Now, let us turn to other kinds of outside interaction which do not necessarily involve members of the same group.

We will consider three variables: interest in community affairs, activity in community affairs, and frequency of informal visiting. Ahead of time, it is hard to know what to expect. It could be that members who are very active in their communities, either in formal organizations or in informal social affairs, would be drawn into competing interests and their presence in the group would lower its cohesion. It could also be that people who are active outside develop skills in group participation which make them assets to the group or it could be that striking a balance between activists and passivists would be the best formula for producing an effective group.

In the original questionnaire, respondents were asked to rate their interest in local politics, civic organizations, national politics, world affairs, and church activities. Our original aim was to divide the members into those with a purely local orientation and those whose interests were in the national and world spheres. The pattern of inter-relationships of the items cast doubt on this distinction, since we found that our "locals" had more national and world interests than did those disinterested in the local scene. That is, our original analysis led to the idea that among Great Books members extra-local interests are a necessary pre-condition for local interests, not a substitute. Therefore, when we look at the

Chart 5.5
Local Interest and Drop-Out

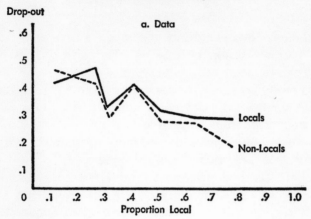

Drop-out

a. Data

Proportion Local

Locals

Non-Locals

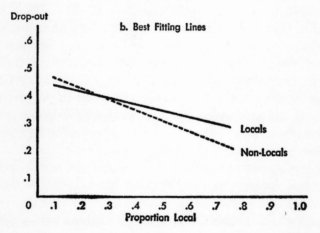

Drop-out

b. Best Fitting Lines

Proportion Local

Locals

Non-Locals

members who were scored as locals, we have a group who tend to report high interest in affairs both in their communities and in the nation and world. Dividing members into local and non-locals, and scoring groups in terms of their proportion local, let us see whether these interests relate to program retention.

This is a standard type II relationship, in which retention

increases with local interest at the group level, but there is no individual level difference. The greater the proportion of members who have high interests, the better the group holds its members. This tends to suggest that the competition hypothesis is false.

Outside interests appear to be effective, but we want to know whether this might be because they affect inside interaction. When we dichotomize groups between those with 40 per cent or more locals versus those with 39 per cent or less, we see that localism tends to be related to activity levels.

Table 5.5—Localism and Activity, Controlling for Contacts and Change in Schools (per cent of groups high on local interest)

Contacts	Schools	Active		Less Active	
+	+	53%	(30)	44%	(18)
+	−	62	(16)	38	(13)
−	+	40	(15)	54	(26)
−	−	62	(21)	52	(33)

Except for the low contact, high change groups, high local interest goes with high activity. Why there is this one exception we do not know, but in spite of it, the relationship is strong enough so that when we control for CAS the original relationship between local interest and retention evaporates.

Table 5.6—Local Interest and Drop-Out, Controlling for CAS (per cent drop-out)

Controls	Activity	Schools	PROPORTION LOCAL 0-.39		.40 or More	
+	+	−	21%	(48)	18%	(113)
+	+	+	24	(136)	27	(176)
+	−	+	30	(94)	33	(58)
−	+	+	42	(86)	19	(80)
−	+	−	32	(79)	44	(57)
−	−	+	47	(150)	21	(107)
−	−	−	48	(163)	43	(184)
+	−	−	48	(71)	63	(128)

The local interest effect has disappeared; groups with high proportions of locals have high drop-outs in four comparisons and lower drop-outs in four comparisons. Activity still holds, high activity groups having better retention in seven out of eight comparisons, and change in schools holds in five out of eight comparisons, a figure which would worry us if it were not that two of the three exceptions are due to the difference between the ++— and +++ types, an exception we have noted all along.

In short, groups with high proportions of locally interested have higher retention rates, but apparently only because high local interest facilitates high activity.

Our second outside interaction measure is that of membership in community organizations other than Great Books, as described in Chapter 2. Since we want to avoid having to call them outer actives to contrast them with inner actives, we will call them joiners and non-joiners. Chart 5.6 shows what happens when we tabulate the drop-out rates of joiners and non-joiners in groups which vary in their proportion of joiners.

The relationships here do not fall in our neat classification. For joiners, retention increases with the proportion of joiners. For non-joiners, however, retention increases as P slides up to .50, but as it moves onto the higher P levels, retention starts to decrease. Thus, we have two different relationships, a linear increase in retention for the joiners, and a curvilinear relationship for non-joiners, the non-joiners showing lowest drop-outs in mixed groups and higher drop-out rates in homogeneous groups. The linear increase for joiners seems sensible if we assume that joiners as a class are more highly skilled in group participation, and that therefore their presence in large numbers adds to the skill level of the group. Why the non-joiners show a curvilinear relationship is unknown. Perhaps they benefit from the presence of joiners up to a certain point, but beyond that feel uncomfortable in the presence of so many people who are skillful in interpersonal relations. However, we should note that despite the large number of complicated relationships in these data, we have

Chart 5.6
Joiners and Drop-Out

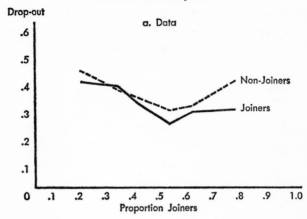

a. Data

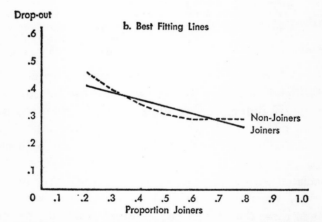

b. Best Fitting Lines

yet to see a compositional effect which indicates that majority-minority position *per se* is important. Therefore, we see no reason why being in a minority on community participation should affect drop-out when being in a minority on other variables doesn't seem to effect retention.

Group level joining rates have very strong relationships with our other variables, and it will be necessary to consider statistical controls in some detail.

In terms of the CAS variables, groups with high proportions of joiners tend to have very high rates of activity.

**Table 5.7—Proportion Joiners, Outside Contacts, and Change
in Schools (per cent of groups which are high
on proportion joiners)**

a. ACTIVITY

Contacts	Schools	High		Low	
+	+	90%	(30)	53%	(15)
+	−	75	(16)	67	(21)
−	+	89	(18)	58	(26)
−	−	62	(13)	58	(33)

b. CONTACTS

Activity	Schools	High		Low	
+	+	90%	(30)	89%	(18)
+	−	75	(16)	62	(13)
−	+	53	(15)	58	(26)
−	−	67	(21)	58	(33)

c. CHANGE IN SCHOOLS

Contacts	Activity	High		Low	
+	+	90%	(30)	75%	(16)
+	−	53	(15)	67	(21)
−	+	89	(18)	62	(13)
−	−	58	(26)	58	(33)

In each row of Table 5.7a, active groups are more likely
to be high joining groups, and except for the bottom row, the
percentage differences are quite strong in comparison with
similar tables in this report. Thus, regardless of the outside
contacts or changes produced by the discussion, high proportions of joiners, people active in their communities, are
associated with high proportions named as active in the discussion. When we turn to Table 5.7b, outside contacts, we find
that in three out of four cases, groups with many joiners are
more likely to have higher rates of outside contacts, a perfectly reasonable finding. Table 5.7c, though, shows no consistent relationship between joining and change in schools in
these group level data.

Let us see what happens to our relationships when we control for CAS. We will have to control simultaneously for CAS,
individual level joining, two levels of activity among the
joiners, and three levels among the non-joiners.

Table 5.8—Proportion of Joiners and Drop-Out, Controlling for CAS, and Individual Level Joining
(per cent dropping out)

PROPORTION JOINERS			JOINERS		NON-JOINERS		
Contact	Activity	School	0-.39	.40+	0-.39	.40-.69	.70+
+	+	−	- % (9)	9% (76)	35% (23)	22%(46)	- % (5)
+	+	+	- (9)	18 (164)	46 (26)	29 (98)	- (8)
+	−	+	39 (18)	36 (45)	31 (49)	24 (29)	- (4)
−	+	+	- (4)	33 (84)	33 (12)	29 (58)	- (4)
−	+	−	38 (16)	39 (41)	29 (41)	40 (25)	45 (11)
−	−	+	34 (29)	31 (72)	46 (91)	30 (50)	- (5)
−	−	−	55 (31)	31 (116)	52 (105)	45 (80)	- (3)
+	−	−	59 (15)	57 (89)	64 (39)	51 (39)	- (9)

Tables like Table 5.8 should be familiar now, but we can review briefly by saying that comparisons across the rows enable us to look for the effects of joining when CAS is held constant, and comparisons down columns enable us to look for the effects of CAS with joining held constant.

The results seem to be as follows: in terms of joining, the relationship disappears among the joiners (1 comparison favoring high levels of joining, 4 favoring low levels), but among the non-joiners, the relationship holds in seven out of eight comparisons between the 0-.39 and the .40-.69 groups. We have only one cell with enough cases to look at the right side of the curve for non-joiners (that is, to test their increased drop-out at high P levels), but for which it's worth, that cell is consistent with the hypothesis.

When we examine our CAS variables, we find a general increase in drop-out down the columns, although if we had to rely on the data for non-joiners in low joining groups we might be a little discouraged.

Table 5.9—Proportion Joiners and Drop-Out, Controlling for Individual Level Joining and Status Composition
(per cent dropping out)

P Status	P Joiners	JOINERS			NON-JOINERS		
		0-.39	.40-.69	.70+	0-.39	.40-.69	.70+
.50+ (High)		26% (53)	29% (318)	31% (172)	37% (139)	33% (282)	45% (33)
0-.49 (Low)		54 (78)	31 (166)	29 (31)	49 (247)	35 (143)	38 (16)

A somewhat more complicated, but definite pattern emerges when we control for the status level of the group.

Beginning with the non-joiners over on the right-hand side of the table, we see that in both status levels the curvilinear relationship is maintained. Thus, regardless of the variable controlled, non-joiners have a lower drop-out in the middle ranges of P. Among the joiners the picture is unclear. We could say that joiners show an increase in retention as P increases, but only in the low status groups, but we think we can show an alternative interpretation.

Let us look at status. Despite the fact that the status relationship has held in a number of controls, here it does not. When we inspect Table 5.9, we note that when the probability of joining is less than .39 we get quite a strong status difference, based on a reasonable number of cases. In groups with a higher proportion of joiners, however, status shows no consistent effect. What this suggests to us is not that our original status effect was spurious, but rather that status differences only help groups with low proportions of joiners.

Putting it another way, Table 5.9 suggests that again we have an either-or relationship. Program retention will apparently be greater in groups with high proportions of high status people and/or high proportions of joiners. Conversely, retention is lower in groups which have low proportions of high status people and low proportions of joiners. From this point of view it would seem that status composition and numbers of joiners serve equivalent ends, and that groups which have one are not affected by the presence or absence of the other. Since both in our sample and in other studies, high status goes with high activity in the community, the formulation is intuitively agreeable, but what this effect is we do not know. We may speculate that it is probably social and not intellectual, since we still get a status effect when we control for group composition in terms of education and knowledge scores. Beyond this, our data do not shed much light on the matter.

If these conjectures are true, it may be that the strange curves in Chart 5.6 arise because two separate things are going on at the same time: 1) Status composition and proportion joiners together operate to create a favorable climate within the group. 2) Within groups with such a favorable climate joiners seem to be relatively unaffected by the proportion of joiners, but non-joiners have higher drop-out rates when they are mixed in with high or low proportions of joiners.

Although the relationships are complicated, we should note that none of the evidence supports the "competition" hypothesis, and although it probably operates indirectly, Great Books groups seem to benefit from the presence of many members who are also interested and involved in other local groups and organizations; the only exception is the handful of non-joiners in groups with high proportions of joiners, these representing about 3 per cent of the participants in our sample. In comparison, about 20 per cent of the sample participants are in the low status, low joining groups, which average about 50 per cent drop-out, as compared with drop-out rates in the 30 per cent-40 per cent range for most groups with a favorable climate.

Finally, we turn to pure sociability, the frequency of informal visiting. Our original questionnaire asked, "About how many evenings per month (on the average) do you spend in informal visiting and entertaining?" and individuals are divided into those who spend 5 or more (sociable) versus those who report fewer nights per month; with groups arrayed in terms of their proportion sociable. Tabulating all of this against drop-out, we get Chart 5.7.

Regardless of its meaning, Chart 5.7 is a pretty thing to behold. We get two nice curves, parallel to each other, and a sharper "curvy-ness" than we have yet seen. At most P levels, the *less* sociable have slightly higher drop-out rates (another blow to the competition hypothesis), but within a given category, we find a curvilinear relationship, drop-outs

Chart 5.7
Sociability and Drop-Out

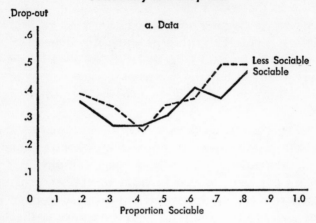

a. Data

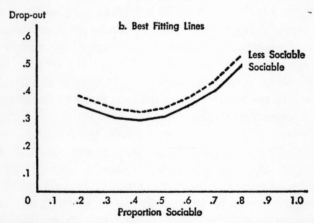

b. Best Fitting Lines

being fewest where about half of the group are sociable, with higher attrition among groups low on sociability, and much higher attrition among groups with extremely high proportions of sociable members.

Moderation in all things, as Aristotle advises, may not apply to most of our variables, but here the data suggest that moderate sociability is a good omen in terms of program retention. Could it be that groups with unsociable people lack the ease of interaction necessary for active discussions, while among groups of very sociable people their high sociability creates "noise" which interferes with serious discussion?

If so, we should find that sociability is related to the CAS variables.

Table 5.10—Sociability, Contacts, Activity, and Change in Schools (per cent of groups high on)

	PROPORTION SOCIABLE		
	0-.29	.30-.59	.60+
Activity	43%	50%	38%
Contacts	34	50	53
Schools	51	54	49
Number of groups	(35)	(84)	(53)

The relationships are different for different variables. Outside contacts, as one would predict, increase steadily with sociability. However, activity, and change in schools are highest in the middle *P* values, and lower at each extreme.

Since activity level is related to outside contacts, let's hold it constant.

Table 5.11—Sociability and Activity, Controlling for Outside Contacts (per cent of groups high on activity)

OUTSIDE CONTACTS	P SOCIABILITY					
	0-.29		.30-.59		.60+	
High	58%	(12)	60%	(42)	50%	(28)
Low	38	(23)	41	(42)	24	(25)

Both types of social relationship contribute to high activity levels. Within each sociability category, groups with high outside contacts are more likely to be high on activity; within each contact level, sociability continues to show a curvilinear relationship with activity.

In order to see whether sociability affects change in schools, we have to hold constant contacts and activity, and this is just too much for our limited number of cases. For the record, however, when one does make such a tabulation, sociability shows no relationship with change in schools, although whether this reflects the real situation or merely attrition of cases, we cannot tell.

We do know enough to wonder whether the curvilinear relationship between sociability and program retention is due to the fact that moderate sociability seems to grease the wheels of the CAS process. Table 5.12 answers this question.

Table 5.12—Sociability Composition and Drop-Out, Controlling for Individual Sociability, Outside Contacts, Activity, and Change in Schools (per cent dropping out)

P SOCIABLE	SOCIABLE						LESS SOCIABLE					
Grouped CAS	0-.29		.30-.59		.60+		0-.29		.30-.59		.60+	
++- & +++	- %	(4)	14%	(99)	23%	(118)	22%	(32)	28%	(135)	29%	(49)
+-+ & -++	-	(9)	17	(70)	51	(63)	28	(36)	21	(97)	60	(25)
-+- & --+	56	(16)	35	(88)	34	(64)	56	(55)	32	(115)	25	(32)
--- & +--	36	(22)	45	(94)	58	(149)	39	(77)	46	(100)	49	(57)

The relationship with sociability appears to vanish, in Table 5.12. Our notion of curvilinearity will make specific predictions about 14 comparisons, but the predictions are correct in only 8 cases, incorrect in 6. CAS is strongly related to sociability, so the relationship between CAS and drop-out is somewhat reduced, but 31 predictions can be made on the basis of CAS (e.g., predicting that the top row will have less drop-out than the second, third, fourth; predicting that the second will have less than the third and fourth, etc.). Of these 24 hold. Thus, CAS appears to have weathered the storm much better than has sociability.

Our inclination would be to infer that moderate levels of sociability have a favorable influence on retention, but only as they operate to raise levels of activity in the group.

In summary, the outside interaction variables are both very strong and quite unimportant factors in program retention. While they do show quite striking zero-order relationships with drop-out when one controls for the other variables in our analysis, their independent contribution is negligible.

1) Program retention increases steadily with the propor-

tion of locally interested people in the group, but this appears to be because such groups have high activity levels.

2) Among joiners program retention increases steadily with the proportion interested in community affairs, while among non-joiners a curvilinear relationship obtains. When, however, one controls for the other variables, some curious results turn up. First, the effect of the proportion joining on joiners disappears, while the curvilinear relationship among non-joiners remains (the only outside interaction variable which contributes independently). Second, the proportion joining appears to work with the proportion high status as alternative effects on the group climate.

3) Program retention has a curvilinear relationship with the proportion of sociable members, retention being highest where about half are sociable, retention being lower at the extremes. The contribution, however, disappears when we hold CAS constant, which suggests that moderate sociability operates to facilitate group activity levels, which, in turn, affect drop-out.

Two more general comments may be made.

First, on the whole, community activity and interest is a favorable sign in Great Books groups. Thus, there is little evidence to support the idea that competition with other community organizations is a significant factor in losses from the discussion groups. In fact, the individual level relationships tend to show that extra-group participation goes with higher retention.

Second, it does not appear that pure frequency of outside interaction is the variable here, since we get different patterns of relationship with community interests and memberships than we get with informal visiting. Roughly speaking, it appears that high levels of serious outside interaction are a good sign, but beyond a certain point, high levels of sociability are a bad sign. Perhaps one of the key factors in Great Books is that it focuses on serious social interaction. Groups whose members have a limited range of social interaction do poorly, but so do groups with high amounts of non-serious social interaction. It is groups composed of people characterized by high rates of participation in serious affairs that seem to do particularly well.

§ Summary

Because some of the relationships reported in the next chapter will modify our conclusions, we shall defer an extensive summary of compositional effects until the end of Chapter 6. We can, however, plug all the variables we have considered into our model.

In general, then, we can say that while roles in the family and community are important for program retention, they are less likely to be direct contributors than to affect retention through influencing role volume. Status-Joining does appear to be a favorable sign in itself, but sex, marital status, local interest, and moderate sociability all have to be plugged into role volume in the discussion groups before they pay off in increased membership retention.

6. Drop-Out III: Intellectual and Ideological Variables

*I*n listing the ingredients in our recipe for a successful Great Books discussion group, we have so far left out ideas. In a program devoted to the reading and discussion of ideas, it is not unreasonable to assume that ideas play some part in the outcome. As a matter of fact, we have already seen that self-reported changes in ideas and opinions are a favorable part of the retention process. We shall conclude our analysis by considering two aspects of ideas and beliefs. First, we shall look at the effects of a series of measures which tap intellectual abilities, we shall look at the effects of the members' religious and political affiliations and opinions. The first can be thought of as skills in handling of ideas, and compositionally as the pool of skilled labor available for the work of discussion. The second two can be thought of as commitment to value or ideological positions, and compositionally as the number of viewpoints which have spokesmen in the group.

§ Intellectual Characteristics

Generally speaking, high proportions of members who are high on our measures of intellectual ability go with increased member retention. At the same time, this generalization glosses over some rather complicated statistical patterns and blurs the line between those abilities which can be thought of as effects of participation and those which can be thought of as permanent characteristics of the participants.

The prime example of an "effect" characteristic is the knowledge score used in the original study. For present purposes, all we need to remember from Chapter 3 is this: the measure consisted of 31 sketches which purported to tap knowledge of liberal arts (e.g., three surprised-looking angels plummeting from the clouds to suggest Milton's *Paradise Lost*) and respondents who identified large numbers of the pictures were given high scores on knowledge. Rather detailed statistical analysis suggested that, controlling for quite a number of other variables, increased exposure to Great Books leads to higher scores. After dividing the members into high and low scorers (in terms of the sample median) and sorting groups by their proportion of high scores, we can see whether knowledge scores relate to drop-out.

Chart 6.1, like every one of our "effect" measures shows a sort of mangled version of what we have termed a type III or radiating effect. At each P level, low scorers have higher drop-out rates; and although the form is more meandering than classically linear (the points for the high scorers are linear by our tests, but the ones for the low scorers are not), drop-out rates tend to be lower in groups with high proportions of high scorers. There is some hint that there is an optimum point around .50, but no clear parabolic form is suggested. In short, we can add knowledge scores as a further confirmation of our rough generalization that intellectual

Chart 6.1
Knowledge Score and Drop-Out

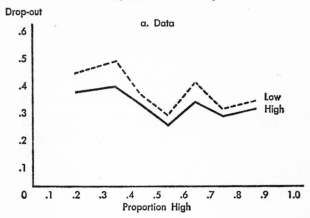

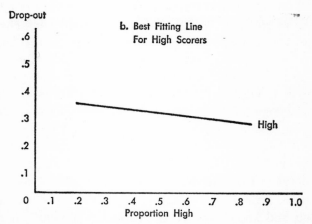

changes and effects have a favorable radiating effect on group retention rates.

In terms of our "Tinkertoy" conceptual model knowledge scores probably belong over on the right side in the group of variables we have called "Intellectual Change." Knowledge scores do have a strong relationship with the other CAS characteristics, and if we dichotomize groups as high or low in proportions of high scorers, we find that the Q measures of association with contacts, activity, and change in schools are .27, .35, and .40, respectively. Thus, as one would expect, this variable shows its strongest relationships on the effect side of our model. We shall not present the detailed data here, but when we control for CAS composition, as in Table 5.4 we find that the group level difference holds in only 11 of the 16 comparisons, which suggests that knowledge scores themselves add little to the CAS process.

The data controlling for knowledge scores do, however, provide some slight reinforcement of our interpretation of the problem of the +— — group, the group with high outside contacts, but low activity and change in schools. We remember that the +— — group had higher loss rates than the — — — groups, although in other CAS comparisons outside contacts were a favorable sign. We suggested that high volume of outside contacts may act to accentuate other effects. That is, in groups with high activity and intellectual changes outside contacts appear to reinforce these factors and to raise retention, but in groups where few people have active roles and few report intellectual changes, outside contacts appear to accentuate the "failure" and to lower retention. If this interpretation is correct, and if knowledge scores belong on the effect side of our scheme, then outside contacts should have a differential effect on groups with high and low knowledge levels.

In order to test this idea, let us consider groups which are all low on Schools and Activity, but which vary in outside contacts and knowledge scores. Table 6.1 presents the data.

Among high scoring individuals the effect is as predicted. Those groups with high knowledge scores benefit from outside contacts, showing a 31 percentage point advantage in retention, while those groups with low knowledge levels suffer from outside contacts, showing a 20 percentage point disadvantage in retention. Among low scoring individuals, the effect is only relative, not absolute. For low scorers in high knowledge groups, outside contacts are again beneficial, but

Table 6.1—Knowledge Levels, Outside Contact Levels, and Drop-Out in Groups Low on Activity and Schools
(per cent dropping out)

KNOWLEDGE		OUTSIDE CONTACTS				
Individual	Group	High		Low		Difference
High	High	14%	(35)*	45%	(82)	−31
	Low	54	(28)	34	(64)	+20
Low	High	24	(21)	47	(43)	−23
	Low	46	(48)	50	(147)	−4

* Number in parentheses is the number of individuals upon whom the percentage is based.

among low scorers in low scoring groups, outside contacts make little or no difference.

Outside contacts are a relatively good omen in high knowledge groups and a relatively bad omen in low knowledge groups, among those discussion groups which are low on activity and schools. If we think of knowledge scores as one of the intellectual changes produced by discussion, we may advance the following hypothesis.

1) In groups which have high activity and high change in schools *and/or* high increase in knowledge, outside contacts lead to greater retention.

2) In groups which have low activity, low change in schools, and low increase in knowledge, outside contacts make no difference or lead to lesser retention.

In short, we would advance the hypothesis (and it is only that) that the CAS process can lead to several different types of intellectual changes, and that if any of them occur, outside contacts are favorable for group retention, but if none of them occur, outside contacts are an unfavorable sign.

Another measure of intellectual prowess is provided by our index of reading quality. We have several different measures of the degree of intellectual challenge of the participants' reading. Since most of them show the same general type of relationship, we shall report on only one, "Level of most worthwhile book." This index was constructed as follows. Each respondent was asked "What book or books—outside of Great Books readings—which you read in the last year impressed you as particularly worthwhile?" The study director provided an impressionistic rating of the degree of intellectual challenge of the books. Respondents were divided into upper-middle or highbrows (readers of Camus, Proust, Strindberg, etc.) and middle brows (readers of James Gould Cozzens, Edna Ferber, Peter Marshall, etc.), no lowbrows being detected by the measuring device. Groups were ordered by their proportion of middlebrows. Chart 6.2 shows the results in terms of drop-out.

Chart 6.2 is the first example we have reported of a type IV, or differential effect relationship. As we noted above, the type IV situation is characterized by a differential impact of group composition on the two sub-classes of individuals. Let's begin with the upper-middle and highbrows, for convenience calling them by the latter term. At each P level, we find that highbrows have a greater retention rate. Thus, people whose outside readings are more in line with their inside readings are more likely to stay in the program. When we examine the line for the highbrows we find little or no variation, and although the best fitting line tips a little, our statistical analysis warns us that we have little reason to believe that the line isn't parallel to the P axis. In sum, highbrows tend, as individuals, to stay with the program and to show little reaction to the reading level of their groups. Middlebrows, however, show a rather strong reaction to composition. We can think of it in either of two ways. The more middlebrows, the greater loss among middlebrows, or the more highbrows the greater the retention of middlebrows. The choice between the two interpretations is perfectly arbitrary, but we rather prefer the latter, if only because it has a sort of optimistic ring. It suggests that although middlebrows are a fairly bad risk, groups with high levels of reading sophistication tend to hold their less sophisticated readers better than those with fewer highbrow readers.

Analysis of the relationships between brow composition

Chart 6.2
Level of Most Worthwhile Book and Drop-Out

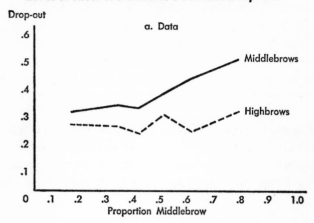

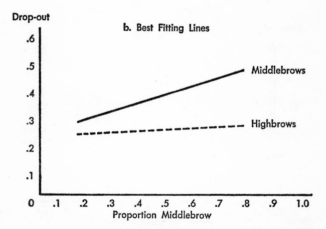

and the other components of our analysis suggests that the reading variable is an independent contributor. That is, the group level Q coefficients between proportion middlebrow and contacts, activity, schools, and status are $-.12$, $.03$, $-.13$, and $-.09$. Since reading composition is essentially independent of the other elements in the scheme, the reading effect is not a function of the relationship of the other elements to drop-out, and we may think of this factor as an independent contributor.

Our final cerebral characteristic is education. In most surveys education is the research worker's best friend. Compared with attitudes and personality characteristics its measurement is quite reliable, and its implications are vague enough so that the survey analyst may interpret its meaning in almost any fashion which seems agreeable: as an indicator of social status, or level of culture, or even native intelligence. Furthermore, it almost always correlates. However, this time, although we get a correlation, the operation of educational composition on Great Books groups turns out to be a very tricky thing indeed. In Chart 6.3, we see the relationships

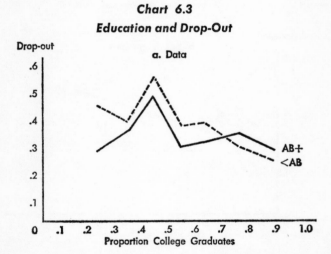

Chart 6.3

Education and Drop-Out

between educational composition, individual education, and drop-out. The respondents are divided into those with the bachelor's degree or more, and those with less than a bachelor's degree, and groups are arranged in terms of their proportion of A.B.'s.

Over-all, with the exception of the very highest *P* levels, we find that drop-out rates are higher among the less educated. This is still another instance of the general finding that the tendency in program retention is "them as has, gets," that is, drop-out is lower among those people and groups which show higher scores on measures of intellectual background, orientation, and skill. However, when we look at the compositional effects, they turn out to be non-linear. For both classes of individuals drop-out rates rise as P increases to around .45 and then decline steadily as P increases beyond .50. The relationship is thus distinctly curvilinear. In Chart 6.3 we have not fitted a smooth curve to the data because the "bend" is too sharp to get a good fit with our standard kit of curves. However, it is clear that the relationships belong to the general family of parabolas.

It would appear that for education, drop-out varies with the homogeneity of the group. Groups which have about a 50-50 split between college graduates and non-college graduates seem to have the worst records; groups with high or low proportions of college graduates seem to do pretty well. Put this way, the suggestion is that while *degree* of "preparation" affects individual drop-out rates, *evenness* of preparation influences group drop-out rates. Before we settle on this hypothesis, however, let us look at the relationships between education and other elements in our model.

We have quite a way to go, but let us start by looking at the relationships between educational composition, and the CAS variables.

Change in Schools is fairly straightforward. In three of the four comparisons high change groups tend to be high education groups, and the one reversal is very small. However, Tables 6.2a and 6.2b are somewhat more complicated. In 6.2a, we notice that in the top two rows active groups are *more* likely to be high education groups, but in the bottom two rows active groups are *less* likely to be high education groups. Likewise, in Table 6.2b, we note that in the first two rows, high contact groups tend to be high education groups, but in the last two rows high contact groups tend to be low

Table 6.2—Group Level Inter-Relations of Contacts, Activity, Change in Schools, and Educational Composition (per cent of groups with .50 or more college graduates)

CONTACTS	SCHOOLS	6.2a ACTIVITY			
		More Active		Less Active	
+	+	87%	(30)	73%	(15)
+	−	81	(16)	67	(21)
−	+	67	(18)	77	(26)
−	−	46	(13)	79	(33)

ACTIVITY	SCHOOLS	6.2b CONTACTS			
		High Contacts		Lower Contacts	
+	+	87%	(30)	67%	(18)
+	−	81	(16)	46	(13)
−	+	73	(15)	77	(26)
−	−	67	(21)	79	(33)

CONTACTS	ACTIVITY	6.2c CHANGE IN SCHOOLS			
		High Change		Lower Change	
+	+	87%	(30)	81%	(16)
+	−	73	(15)	67	(21)
−	+	67	(18)	46	(13)
−	−	77	(26)	79	(33)

education groups. Since the difference between the first two and last two rows in Table 6.2a is a difference in contacts, and the difference between the first two and last two rows in Table 6.2b is a difference in activity, the tables strongly suggest that something complicated is happening. We can see what it is in a much more straightforward fashion, by temporarily ignoring change in schools.

Table 6.3—Education and Activity, Controlling for Contacts (per cent of groups which are high on activity)

	P, Education*	Per Cent	N
	.70+	70	(37)
High Contacts	.50-.69	52	(25)
	.40-.49	38	(8)
	0-.39	33	(12)
	.70+	24	(21)
Low Contacts	.50-.69	30	(43)
	.40-.49	50	(12)
	0-.30	50	(14)

* In this and subsequent tables, P, Education = the proportion of college.

What appears to be happening is this. In high contact groups, activity *increases* with educational level. In low contact groups, activity *decreases* with educational level. The relationship is necessarily symmetrical, so we can reverse the order of the variables and reach the same sort of conclusion.

Table 6.4—Contacts and Activity, Controlling for Education

P, EDUCATION	Q ASSOCIATION BETWEEN CONTACTS AND ACTIVITY	
	Q	N (Groups)
.70+	.76	58
.50-.69	.43	68
.40-.49	−.38	20
0-.39	−.33	26

From this alternative perspective, the results read as follows. Among groups with high educational levels, outside contacts lead to *higher* activity levels; among groups with lower educational levels, outside contacts lead to lower activity. That the difference exists is fairly clear. Why it exists is a matter of speculation. Our speculation would go as follows. Presumably the amount of "intellectualism" in the members' outside contacts differ according to the educational level of the people involved. Among those with college degrees, even though their outside contacts do not approximate those of the eighteenth century salon, the natural patterns of association are likely to involve discussions of ideas, books, plays, etc. When groups of highly educated people then join to discuss the Great Books perhaps they carry over and accentuate patterns of intellectual discussion which already exist outside the group. For the less educated person and group, however, it may be that the intellectual discussions in the program differ considerably from their outside patterns of talk and associations. If so, patterns developed in the outside arena might tend to inhibit free and easy group discussion of intellectual affairs.

Do these findings then imply that our original relationship between educational composition and drop-out can be explained by the relationship between education and the CAS process? No, they do not. Although education has a distinct effect on the workings of the CAS process, by the time the whole thing has ground through, everything is cancelled out. Somewhat more specifically, the cancelling-out mechanism is in the relationship between outside contacts and education.

Table 6.5—Educational Composition and Outside Contacts (per cent of groups which are high on outside contacts)

P, Education	Per Cent	No. of Groups
.70+	64	58
.50-.69	37	68
.40-.49	40	20
0-.39	46	26

There are really too few cases to establish any sort of relationship, but what cases there are suggest that the true relationship may be curvilinear. It certainly would be plausible to think that groups which are homogeneous on education have higher rates of outside contacts, since friends tend to be homogeneous on most social characteristics, and we do notice that the highest percentages of outside contacts are in our extreme P groups, although the differences are small. If this interpretation is valid, it takes some of the sting out of the possibly negative effects of the educational differential. The groups with an educational P of .40-.49 show a negative relationship between outside contacts and activity levels. If, however, they tend to have low rates of outside contacts, the practical effect will be small. That this may be the case, is suggested by the following.

Table 6.6—Educational Composition and Activity (per cent of groups which are high on activity)

P, Education	Per Cent	No. of Groups
.70+	53	58
.50-.69	38	68
.40-.49	45	20
0-.39	42	26

There is no consistent pattern, although the groups with the highest proportions of college graduates do seem to have high activity levels, as one would expect from the individual level association between education and activity.

It appears that heterogeneity in educational composition may contribute independently toward drop-out rates, since, although educational composition is heavily involved in *how* CAS operates, it does not seem involved in the distribution of CAS. In order to demonstrate this, however, we need to examine drop-out rates, controlling simultaneously for individual education, educational composition, and CAS composition.

Table 6.7—Drop-Out, Individual Education, Educational Composition, and Grouped CAS (per cent dropping out)

			NON-COLLEGE GRADUATES			COLLEGE GRADUATES		
				P, Education			P, Education	
Contact	Activity	School	0-.39	.40-.49	.50+	0-.39	.40-.49	.50+
+	+	−	26% (23)	71% (14)	26% (100)	0% (10)	64% (11)	19% (305)
+	+	+						
+	−	+	31 (54)	43 (21)	31 (64)	46 (24)	24 (17)	28 (130)
−	+	+						
−	+	−	24 (41)	53 (45)	36 (81)	6 (16)	53 (36)	36 (153)
−	−	+						
−	−	−	73 (55)	60 (35)	48 (124)	57 (21)	52 (27)	44 (255)
+	−	−						

Attempting to control simultaneously for two types of individuals, three types of educational compositions, and eight types of CAS compositions leaves us with too few cases in most cells to be of any use. We can improve the situation a little by combining CAS types into four pairs, but, even so, the crucial cells run too thin to draw firm conclusions. This in itself is probably the most important finding, for we note that of the 1662 respondents in Table 6.7, 73 per cent are in groups with P values of .50 or higher, 15 per cent are in groups with P values of .39 or less, and only 12 per cent are in the danger zone from .40 to .49. Thus, from a practical point of view it is necessary to stress that educational heterogeneity is not a major problem in Great Books retention. However, in terms of a more abstract understanding of how these groups work, the effect of educational composition is a very interesting one.

Taking Table 6.7 variable by variable, we notice the following—in nine out of twelve comparisons, individuals with bachelor's degrees have lower drop-out rates than individuals with less than a college degree, and they are higher in only one comparison thus corroborating our belief that on the whole education is a favorable sign, in terms of individual characteristics. In terms of educational composition, sixteen comparisons are possible, and in twelve of them the .40-.49 group has a higher drop-out rate. In five out of eight comparisons between .40-.49 and 0-.39, the former have a higher drop-out rate. Somewhat more consistently, in seven out of eight comparisons the .40-.49 groups have higher drop-out rates than the .50+ groups, and the single reversal is only four percentage points. Thus, while the advantage of the 0-.39 groups over the fearsome forties may be spurious (or the number of cases in these cells may be too small to justify any serious conclusions) the advantage of the high P groups is probably not an artifact of CAS. Finally, we note that in the .50+ comparisons our CAS order holds up well, although in the other compositional groups it is spotty, either because of the effect of the educational composition, or more probably because of the small number of cases per cell.

In short, we actually have too few cases to draw any firm conclusion, but on the whole we find that we cannot get rid of the educational effect by controlling for CAS, and, on the whole, it appears as if educational heterogeneity is an independent factor in the retention process.

In Great Books, as elsewhere, education is correlated with social status. When we dichotomize groups as high and low on these two proportions, we find a Q association of .64, which is the highest degree of association among any of our P values.

Therefore, we must examine social status and education simultaneously, before we draw any more arrows on our model.

Table 6.8—Status Composition, Educational Composition, Education, and Drop-Out (per cent dropping out)

P, STATUS	NON-GRADUATES						COLLEGE GRADUATES					
	0-.39		.40-.49		.50+		0-.39		.40-.49		.50+	
.50+	27	(44)	50	(46)	35	(240)	33	(18)	37	(38)	30	(612)
0-.49	47	(129)	59	(69)	38	(129)	34	(53)	57	(53)	34	(231)

Table 6.8, for a change, is rather simple. In each of the six comparisons drop-out rates are lower in the high status groups; in each of the four comparisons, the relationship between educational composition and drop-out is curvilinear, and in five out of six comparisons, non-graduates have higher drop-out rates than college graduates. Thus, we conclude that status and educational composition contribute to group retention independently. Similar analyses led to the same conclusions regarding involvement in community organizations.

It is not easy to summarize the effect of intellectual variables as a group, since each behaves in a different fashion, and the fashions tend toward the more complicated types of relationships in our classification. On the whole, the net effect of intellectual characteristics is clearly favorable at the individual level. That is, at most of the relevant P levels, there are fewer drop-outs among high quiz scorers, the highbrow readers, and the college educated. However, in terms of group effects, the three characteristics behave in different ways. Knowledge scores generally, although not without exception, are a favorable sign in terms of composition. High proportions of highbrows are helpful, but mostly to the non-highbrows in the group.

The findings on education are extremely complicated, perhaps even polymorphous perverse. Let us review them in detail.

1) Within groups of a given membership composition, college graduates are somewhat more likely to stay with the program than non graduates.

2) There is some evidence that educational heterogeneity,

i.e. groups with 40 to 49 per cent college graduates, lowers retention.

3) Practically speaking, because of the high educational levels of the members and the fact that the difference between the 40 to 49 per cent groups and the 0 to 39 per cent groups is dubious, the most important conclusion is that groups with majorities of college graduates do well.

4) Education plays an important role in the CAS process. It does so in two different ways. First, as Chapter 3 demonstrated, at the level of individuals, high education leads to high activity. Second, educational composition and outside contacts interact to affect activity levels. Among groups with majorities of college graduates, high rates of inter-personal contacts outside the group go with high levels of role activity in the group. Among groups with minorities of college graduates, high rates of inter-personal contacts outside the group go with low levels of activity in the discussion.

These findings have two implications. From the practical point of view they suggest that high education is favorable for group continuity, both in terms of the individual level relationship, and in terms of the group level relationship at P values of .50 and above.

From a more general sociological viewpoint these data cast more light on the "intrinsic" "extrinsic" hypotheses of role structure discussed in Chapter 3. In Chapter 3 we found that age and size of the groups showed no relationship with role volume, but that individual characteristics such as intellectual ability, sex, and marital status were related to activity. At that time we suggested that the data supported the idea that the role systems in Great Books groups do not arise out of the exigencies of interaction in the discussion, but are heavily influenced by the carry-over into small groups of role propensities developed in the outside world. At that time we also noted some compositional effects on activity, but postponed their discussion. Our findings on education provide an opportune moment for that discussion. Our data seem to show that the larger social world affects role structures in these small groups in two ways. First, as we saw in Chapter 3 it would seem that there is some direct transfer of outside role habits to the discussions. The second way, apparently is through a social climate effect.

We tend to think of the "small group" in terms of the experimental small group in which strangers are brought together under laboratory conditions. In empirical reality, however, there is considerable inter-locking of group memberships, particularly in educational and voluntary organizations. In school rooms, PTA's, scout troops, bridge clubs, churches, businesses, and some professional relationships—that is, in organizational contexts which command only a limited portion of their members' time, we typically find people who see each other "outside" as well as "inside." It is our impression that the insulation between these contexts is often very thin.

As Parsons has noted, professional ethics and codes of business practice can be seen as attempts to create just such insulation. Where, as in Great Books, there is no "ethical" problem involved, it appears to us that there is considerable influence from outside to inside. (It could well be that the influence goes the other way too, and Great Books relationships affect the outside relationships of the members, but we have no data on this.) If group educational composition is interpreted as an index of the intellectual climate of the outside relationships, it would appear that this climate is very important to the groups. Those groups with a strong web of outside interaction appear to carry over into Great Books the values or role relationships of the outside. Where, as in the case of highly educated groups, these outside relationships jibe with the values and roles of the program, they reinforce it. Where, however, this outside climate of interaction is not congruent with the practices and values of Great Books, it apparently dampens the process through lowering the volume of role participation. Either way, the analysis suggests that Great Books groups are strongly affected by the ways in which they inter-lock with the social worlds of their members.

We can now up-date our model as follows.

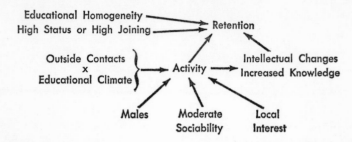

We have added educational homogeneity as an independent contributor (not including reading level because it doesn't affect individuals uniformly), added increased knowledge to the effect side, and indicated that educational composition affects the contact-activity mechanism as well as affecting drop-out directly.

Although the differences are not always consistent, most of our intellectual variables seem to show an individual level difference which leads us to the not astounding conclusion that the more able are more likely to stay with the program. What is somewhat more interesting, however, is the pattern which turns up when we begin to look at several measures of intellectual ability simultaneously. Let us begin with scores on our test of liberal arts knowledge.

To begin with, knowledge scores are associated with years of exposure to the program and with role activity, both of which play a part in individual level retention. When we control for exposure, activity, and also age, the relationship remains. However, a part of the zero order difference does come from exposure, for when one controls for exposure the relationship between knowledge score and drop-out, although consistent, is rather small.

Similarly, the relationship between formal educaton and

drop-out can not be explained away by the relationships between age and activity and education. However, let us see what happens when we look at the simultaneous effects of knowledge scores and formal education.

Table 6.9—Formal Education, Knowledge Score, and Drop-Out (per cent dropping out)

| QUIZ | EDUCATION | | | |
	Less than College Graduate		College Graduate	
High	28%	(239)	28%	(601)
Low	41	(387)	32	(387)

The relationship appears to be asymmetrical. Among non-college graduates, knowledge scores produce a 13 per cent difference, but among college graduates only 4 per cent. Or, reading the table the other way, among high scorers, formal education makes no difference, but among low scorers, education makes a 9 per cent difference. What this suggests is that these two measures of ability are not additive. Rather, people who are in a favorable position on one or both have the same drop-out rates, which are somewhat lower than among those who possess neither.

What happens when we add a third measure of intellectual ability? Let us consider a measure of ability to judge poetry, based on an instrument developed by Trabue and Abbott.[1] These authors collected a number of classic poems and constructed damaged versions of brief selections from each. They developed for each poem: (a) a sentimentalized version, (b) a version which was flattened to make it "matter-of-fact," and (c) a metrically damaged version. The final result was a set of poems which could be used to test a respondent's ability to distinguish a poem of acknowledged excellence from a vulgarized version.

In the following table we see the simultaneous effects of knowledge scores, formal education, and poetry scores, di-

1. M. R. Trabue and Allen Abbott, "A Measure of Ability to Judge Poetry," *Teacher's College Record*, Vol. XXII (1921).

chotomized at the median. Age is controlled in the table, essentially to show that the pattern of intellectual abilities is not involved in our age difference in retention, younger members being more likely to drop out in seven out of eight comparisons.

Table 6.10—Poetry Score, and Per Cent Dropped Out

KNOWLEDGE	COLLEGE GRADUATE	Age						
		UNDER 35			35 OR OLDER		
		High	Low	Differ-ence	High	Low	Differ-ence
High	Yes	36% (91)	31% (169)	−5	29% (115)	23% (225)	−6
High	No	24 (21)	28 (32)	4	38 (52)	24 (129)	−14
Low	Yes	34 (35)	40 (110)	6	28 (58)	28 (179)	0
Low	No	39 (36)	54 (91)	15	31 (51)	36 (204)	5

Poetic sensitivity, at least as measured by our test, does not contribute consistently. In four comparisons the better poets are more likely to stay, in one there is no difference, and in three comparisons the better poets are more likely to drop-out. There is an interesting pattern in the table, though. If we think of the percentage difference in drop-out rates for high and low poetry scores as an index of the effect of poetry, and if we think of the rows in the table as an index of intellectual ability in terms of education and liberal arts knowledge, it looks as if the effect of poetic skill is negatively related to the respondent's level of preparation on other variables. For high scoring college graduates poetry shows a slight negative relationship with retention, for low scoring non-college graduates it shows a slight positive effect, and in-between it is in-between. Just as college degrees only helped low knowledge scorers, poetry seems to help (in terms of retention) those who are both low on knowledge test and are not college graduates. Among the best prepared its effect, if any, is deleterious.

Perhaps an even more complicated pattern is beginning to emerge. It might be that a given measure of ability only helps those who are unprepared in other areas and even hurts those who are highly prepared in other areas. In order to test this new idea, let us now add a fourth measure, musical sophistication. The items were selected from a larger set of musical titles chosen so as to cover a range of musical sophistication ranging from the lower middlebrow (*The 1812 Overture*) through upper middle brow (Beethoven's *Archduke Trio*) to high brow (Palestrina's *Missa Papae Marcelli*). The entire set of 13 items produced a nice Guttman musical scale when respondents were asked to rate the items in terms of familiarity, although here we shall merely dichotomize them into highs and lows.

One would not expect musical sophistication to relate to retention because the curriculum of the program is rather tone deaf. However, we get the same pattern when we introduce musical sophistication into the complex of intellectual variables. If we dichotomize each of the measures—education, knowledge score, poetry, and music, we can count the number of intellectual measures on which a given respondent has a favorable score. Then we can see the effect of a given variable on respondents who are high on different numbers of other intellectual measures. Table 6.11 presents the results of this analysis.

Table 6.11—Effects of Education, Knowledge Scores, Poetry, and Musical Sophistication on Retention of Respondents with Varying Scores on Other Variables in the Set (percentage difference)

NUMBER OF OTHER VARIABLES ON WHICH RESPONDENT IS HIGH	VARIABLE			
	Knowledge	Education	Poetry	Music
3	−13	−7	−10	−4
1-2	7	3	1	2
0	27	15	12	12

Table 6.11 may be read as follows. Among respondents who were high on education, poetry, and music, there was a 13 per cent difference in drop-out between high and low knowledge scorers, the highs dropping out more often; among respondents low on knowledge poetry, and music,

there was a 15 per cent difference in drop-out rates between college graduates and non-college graduates, the non-college graduates dropping out more often.

The pattern is the same for each variable. Among respondents low on everything else, high scores on a given variable boost retention; among respondents high on everything else, high scores on a given variable lower retention, and among respondents in between, high scores have only a small effect.

The implication here is that the relationship between intellectual abilities and drop-out may be curvilinear. Respondents who have no area of intellectual strength have rather high drop-out rates, respondents strong in a few areas do well, but respondents who have strengths in a wide variety of intellectual areas are not as good risks as those in the middle. As a rough test of this idea let us look at drop-out rates according to the number of intellectual measures on which the respondent is high.

Table 6.12—Number of Intellectual Measures Upon Which Respondent Is a High Scorer and Drop-Out
(per cent dropping out)

Number	Per Cent	N
0	47	184
1	31	384
2	32	137
3	26	351
4	34	115

The differences are not striking, but we do see an increase in retention as scores increase from zero to three, while among those high on all four items drop-out rates are higher. If this curvilinear hypothesis is accepted, two interpretations come to mind. On the one hand, it could be that each of these measures is tapping a single general dimension of intellectual sophistication, and those with scores of four are over-prepared. On the other, it could be that these are measures of quite different intellectual areas (the effect of music here is consistent with this idea) and the high scorers are not "better," just more diverse in their interests, some of which lead them away from the program.

We cannot answer the question with any certainty, but we do have one piece of evidence which supports the "quality" rather than "diversity" interpretation. This evidence comes from re-examination of our data on reading already reported in terms of its compositional effects.

Table 6.13 shows the relationship between reading level and retention, controlling for age, education, and knowledge score. Similar results turn up when we control for activity and exposure.

Table 6.13—Reading Quality Index and Drop-Out, Controlling for Age, Education, and Knowledge Score
(per cent dropping out)

AGE	EDUCATION	KNOWLEDGE SCORE	PROPORTION MORE DIFFICULT					
			All		Some		None	
Under 35	Less than BA	Low	68	(19)	44	(18)	48	(46)
		High	30	(10)	21	(24)	-	(8)
	BA and more	Low	35	(23)	23	(22)	59	(34)
		High	40	(50)	32	(77)	30	(66)
35 and older	Less than BA	Low	24	(21)	18	(39)	48	(67)
		High	41	(41)	19	(37)	27	(41)
	BA and more	Low	21	(19)	22	(41)	37	(63)
		High	23	(57)	23	(96)	33	(84)

We notice that in six out of eight possible comparisons, the "all difficult" readers have higher drop-out rates than the "Some," while in six out of seven comparisons the "Nones" have higher drop-out rates than the "Somes." Thus, drop-out rates tend to have a sort of curvilinear relationship with the "brow level" of the outside reading.

The evidence is neither entirely consistent nor terribly strong in terms of strength of correlations, but we would draw the following general conclusions about relationships between intellectual preparation and program retention.

First, those members who are the very least prepared, who are toward the bottom on every measure, are a high risk group in terms of retention, presumably because they are not up to the readings or active participation in the discussions.

Second, the precise intellectual skills involved are varied. It appears sufficient for a member to have some skill in poetic sensitivity, liberal arts knowledge, musical sophistication, or formal college training, but it doesn't make a lot of difference which it is.

Third, extremely high levels of preparation may also lead to slightly higher drop-outs. The difference is less than the difference between none and some, and it would be more conservative to say that beyond a certain point additional background doesn't add to retention. However, there is some evidence for a curvilinear relationship.

Pragmatically speaking, however, it may be that intellectual preparation is not a practical problem for the program. Thus, 60 per cent of the members are college graduates, and among the remainder a number are high on our other indexes. In Table 6.12, only 16 per cent of the members scored zero, and their drop-out rates were only about 15 per cent higher than those scoring 1 or more. Thus, roughly speaking, only about 15 per cent of 16 per cent or about 2 per cent of the members may be thought of as lost due to lack of intellectual background. Similarly, only 10 per cent scored four on the index and their drop-out rate is only slightly higher than those scoring one through three. Thus, in the nature of things Great Books tends to recruit people in that span of intellectual ability which is favorable for retention.

One may hazard the guess, however, that if the program sought to expand to a conspicuously less prepared audience, losses due to low levels of preparation might increase considerably.

Ironically, the variable which should be simple and straightforward—intellectual ability—has produced the most complicated and inconsistent results. At the compositional level, our three measures, knowledge score, reading level, and education, each produce complex and different forms of relationship. At the individual level, the relationships are slight and there is indirect evidence that the effects are curvilinear. In terms of general conclusions, all we can draw are negative ones. There is no evidence that the program is "too hard" for the members it now recruits, and what evidence there is suggests that only a small proportion find it too easy. Since the educational effect and the individual level intellectual effects are curvilinear, one may suggest that the current situation is fairly good, in that the program tends to recruit high proportions of college graduates, but not high proportions of super high brows. All we can really advance as a speculation is that a strong shift toward recruitment of even better prepared people or of even less prepared people might have negative consequences for retention.

We have added educational homogeneity and reading level as independent contributors, added increased knowledge to the effect group, and indicated that educational composition affects the contacts-activity mechanism, as well as retention, *per se*.

Let us now turn to the consideration of a new set of variables, ideological positions.

§ Ideological Positions

Just as the Great Books groups discuss religion and politics, in this section of our report we want to discuss religion and politics as factors in program retention. We can group them together and set them apart from the other variables because these are a type of membership in which ideological and value considerations are at the forefront. When we sort out members in terms of their party allegiance or religious affiliation, we can be sure that they will differ in their opinions on many of the readings. Thus, the results we get will shed some light on the role of diversity of values in group discussion.

Chart 6.4
Political Preference and Drop-Out

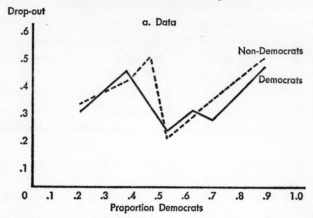

In terms of political party preference, as Chapter 2 indicated, we found a fairly equal division between the major parties, 48 per cent Democrats, 41 per cent Republicans, and 10 per cent independents. In order to simplify our analysis, independents are combined with Republicans, so that each member can be scored as a Democrat or non-Democrat, and each group scored in terms of its proportion of Democrats. Chart 6.4 summarizes the relationship with drop-out.

The most important and only unambiguous conclusion here is that there are no simple linear relationships. There is no individual level difference between Democrats and non-Democrats in their drop-out rates. Likewise there is no simple increase or decrease in drop-out as the proportion of Democrats varies. This suggests that political position or orientation in itself is unimportant for program retention. Despite certain speculations voiced about the curriculum of the program, we see no tendency for either national political persuasion to cling tenaciously or abandon ship.

At the same time, it appears that the blend or mix of political position within the group is an important factor. In the .50-.59 group we find a low drop-out rate near 20 per cent and at around .35 and .85 we find high rates near 50 per cent. The form of the function is one which is not in our tidy catalogue, and it is difficult to draw any conclusion. One way of looking at it might be as follows—the low drop-out rates are near the .50-.50 mark, or where "sides" are about equal, while the high drop-out rates occur in groups split into majority, minority subgroups. One may speculate that equal division on politics would tend to result in vigorous discussion, while an unequal division would result in the majority dominating the minority and neither subgroup feeling that a fair opportunity for discussion had been achieved.

If this speculation has any merit, we should see some sort of relationship between political composition and the CAS mechanism, which we have hypothesized as a process for developing vigorous discussion and intellectual changes. We do not have enough cases to pay any attention to the lower drop-out rates below .30, so we will merely contrast the .50-.59 group with the other types containing more and fewer Democrats. The former group we will call politically diverse, the latter politically homogeneous.[2]

Let us now see whether diversity relates to outside contacts, activity, and change in schools.

Table 6.14—Political Composition, Contacts, Activity, and Change in Schools

PER CENT OF GROUPS WHICH ARE HIGH ON	PROPORTION DEMOCRAT		
	0-.49	.50-.69	.70+
Outside Contacts	47%	40%	62%
Activity	40	51	47
Change in Schools	46	60	53
Number of groups	(85)	(55)	(32)

Comparing the diverse 50's with their homogeneous neighbors, we see some differences. The diverse groups are higher

2. The terminology here is, we admit, a little deceptive. Actually, of course, groups with P's of .30-.49 are just as diverse as groups with P's of .50-.69, from a formal mathematical point of view. By diversity we really refer to slight Democratic majorities, since the .30-.49 groups have quite high drop-out rates.

on change, higher on activity, but lower on outside contacts. The differences are slight, but they suggest that further mining may be profitable.

Remembering that, on the whole, high rates of outside contacts lead to high activity, and noting that diverse groups are slightly higher on activity and slightly lower on outside contacts, let us look at political composition, outside contacts, and activity.

Table 6.15—Outside Contacts, Political Diversity, and Activity (per cent of groups high on activity)

OUTSIDE CONTACTS	POLITICAL TYPE			
	Diverse		Homogeneous	
High	55%	(22)	57%	(60)
Low	48	(33)	26	(57)

There is a fair difference in Table 6.15, and we have two alternative ways of interpreting it. On the one hand, we can say that political composition seems to affect activity differently in high and low outside contact groups. In groups with high outside contacts, political diversity makes no difference at all. In low contact groups, however, diversity appears to lead to higher activity. This makes a certain amount of sense. For group members who already know each other well, political diversity is probably only one of a large number of social characteristics which affect their relations with each other. However, for the low outside contact groups, political diversity may provide the spark necessary to get a vigorous discussion going.

An alternative, but not contradictory, formulation is to say that groups will have high activity rates if the members know each other well and/or are politically diverse. Conversely, a group will have a low activity rate if it is politically homogeneous *and* is low on social bondedness.

In short, it appears that political composition, like education, intervenes in the contacts-activity corner of our model.

Therefore, it is incumbent upon us to consider education here.

Table 6.16—Education, Outside Contacts, Political Composition, and Per Cent of Groups High on Activity

OUTSIDE CONTACTS	P, EDUCATION			
	0-.49		.50+	
	Diverse	Homogeneous	Diverse	Homogeneous
High	—% (2)	39% (18)	60% (20)	64% (42)
Low	78 (9)	35 (17)	38 (24)	22 (40)

The number of variables is breathing down the neck of the number of cases, but we can learn a little more from Table 6.16 than we could by speculating about what might happen. To begin with we note that our conclusions about the relations among outside contacts, political diversity, and activity are unchanged. If we look at the bottom row of Table 6.16 we see that in both educational levels, there is more activity among diverse groups in those groups with low outside contacts. Among the high contact groups, however, there is no relationship in the only educational level with enough cases to examine.

How about our previous finding that the relationship between contacts and activity reverses direction in different educational types? In the high educational levels, we certainly see that high contacts relate to high activity, for in both political types in highly educated groups there is a strong difference between the rows. We just don't have enough cases to tell much in the low education group. However, another inference suggests that the reversal is there. Let us look at low contact groups (the bottom row of Table 6.16), and compare groups which have the same political type. We notice that among low contact groups, activity is higher in the low education category. However, when we turn to the top row, we note that the opposite is true. The high education groups both have higher activity percentages than the single low education cell with enough cases to percentage. Thus, although we can't tell whether the correlation between activity and contacts reverses in the low education groups, we do see that the correlation between education and activity reverses in different contact groups, which amounts to the same thing.

We can now sum up our findings on variables which intervene in the contacts-activity process.

1) Over-all, high rates of outside contacts lead to higher proportions of members active in the discussion.

2) When, however, one controls for educational composition, one finds that in high education groups contacts lead to activity, but in low education groups, outside contacts appear to inhibit activity, inference (1) being a spurious function of the fact that most Great Books groups have high proportions of A.B.'s.

3) Political composition plays little role among the high contact groups, but among low contact groups, political diversity appears to be associated with high activity, regardless of the educational level.

One might speculate that if one had a free hand in arranging the composition of these discussion groups, the best strategies to maximize activity might be as follows.

1) If most of the members will be college graduates, try to arrange groups among people who already know each other, and ignore their political composition.

2) If most of the members will be non-college graduates, try to arrange groups of people who are strangers to each other *and* have slight majorities of Democrats.

Our final question about political composition and CAS is whether diversity has any relationship with change in schools, other than that accounted for by its role as an energizer of discussion activity in the low contact groups. The answer is maybe.

Table 6.17—Political Diversity and Change in Schools, Controlling for Outside Contacts and Activity (per cent of groups which are politically diverse)

Outside Contacts	Activity	High Change		Low Change	
+	+	37%	(30)	6%	(16)
+	−	33	(15)	24	(21)
−	+	50	(18)	55	(13)
−	−	31	(26)	27	(33)

The difference holds in three out of four rows, but is only striking in the top row, hence, we would be loath to draw any conclusion beyond noting that political diversity certainly does not lower change in schools and may raise it a little.

We are now ready to ask whether political diversity contributes to program retention independently, or only through its influence on the CAS process.

Table 6.18—Political Diversity and Drop-Out, Controlling for CAS (per cent dropping out)

Control	Activity	Schools	Diverse		Homogeneous		Per Cent Diverse	N
+	+	−	25%	(12)	18%	(149)	6%	16
+	+	+	21	(93)	27	(219)	37	30
+	−	+	25	(53)	34	(99)	33	15
−	+	+	15	(84)	46	(82)	50	18
−	+	−	27	(81)	51	(55)	55	13
−	−	+	29	(85)	37	(172)	31	26
−	−	−	39	(92)	48	(255)	27	33
+	−	−	30	(30)	63	(169)	24	21

Table 6.18 is really two tables in one. On the right side we see the relationship between political diversity (by which we must remember we mean slight Democratic majorities) and the CAS types, computed at the group level. The relationship is curvilinear. CAS types with very high or very low drop-out rates tend to be homogeneous, while types with average drop-out rates tend to be disproportionately politically diverse.

The left side of the table tells us about individual dropouts. The story is fairly simple. In all but one of the comparisons members of diverse groups have lower drop-out rates, regardless of the CAS type. Within a political composition type, we find that the CAS drop-out order holds pretty well among the homogeneous groups, but among the diverse groups the effects are reduced. Among the diverse groups the highest drop-outs are toward the bottom of Table 6.18, but the differences are small. However, when we apply our comparison count, we find that out of eight possible comparisons, the contact difference holds in six instances, activity in six, and change in schools in seven, thus over-all we can not say that political composition washes out the CAS effects.

In terms of the other components of our model, we find that political composition, when dichotomized in terms of diverse versus homogeneous groups, is not associated with status level, and has a slight negative relationship with educational heterogeneity. Thus, the effect we find cannot be explained by a strong relationship with another independent contributor, and we are ready to add political composition to our group level effects.

However, we should note that we are adding it without any full understanding of how it really works. We are tempted to believe that diversity in political opinion is a favorable characteristic among the Great Books discussion groups. However, if this were the perfect explanation, we would find low drop-outs among the .30-.49 P values, which, in truth, have very high drop-out rates. Thus, the inference must be limited to concluding that slight Democratic majorities have a favorable effect on group retention.

If diversity in politics is a good sign, does it then follow that diversity in religion is also? One is tempted to suggest this hypothesis, but we should remember that although we have grouped these two variables together they differ considerably. In politics one agrees to disagree, and one of the major faiths of Americans is in the legitimacy of the two party system. When it comes to religion, despite great tolerance in this nation, there is probably less conviction that differences in religion are merely a matter of taste and preference. With this alibi in mind, let us turn to the data.

In Chapter 2 we noted that 62 per cent of the participants are Protestant, 15 per cent Jewish, 12 per cent "None," 10 per cent Catholic, and 1 per cent Other. This distribution is very much like that found in surveys of the adult population who have one or more years of college, although Great Books may have some excess of "Nones" and Jews, and a slight deficit in Catholics.

In terms of groups, we get the following distribution.

Table 6.19—Religious Composition of Groups*

	N		Per Cent of All Groups
One Religion Only		25	14
All Protestant	23		13
All Jewish	2		1
All Catholic	0		
Two Religions Only		51	29
Protestant and None	21		12
Protestant and Catholic	14		8
Protestant and Jewish	11		6
Jewish and None	4		2
Catholic and None	1		1
Three Religions Only		53	31
Protestant, Catholic, None	24		14
Protestant, Jewish, None	17		10
Protestant, Catholic, Jewish	12		7
Protestant, Catholic, Jewish, None		43	25
Total		172	99

* The handful of "other" religions have been excluded from this classification.

Although detailed statistical analysis indicates that the groups are much more homogeneous on religion than chance would predict (it also indicates that they are much more homogeneous than chance would predict on almost any variable you can name), there is considerable religious diversity in the groups, only 14 per cent of the groups being of one single religious position, and 25 per cent of the groups including at least one spokesman of each of the four positions in question. We note, however, that not all types of mixtures occur with considerable frequency. Thus, only 5 groups (3 per cent of the groups in the sample) include a mixture of religions, but have no Protestants. Hence, the diversity of composition is essentially that of different mixtures of non-Protestants in groups which have one or more Protestants, 93 per cent of the groups having one or more Protestant members. This asymmetry is going to turn out to be of some importance in considering religious composition.

The simplest test of what may be dignified by the title of the diversity hypothesis is to count the number of religious positions in each group and then look at the drop-out rates in groups which vary in this number. That is, for the moment we will not work with proportions, but rather, assume that the presence of one or more members of a given faith (or non-faith) enables that position to have a hearing. Obviously, the situation will vary with the personalities and numbers of spokesmen, but this simple index provides a good beginning point for our analysis. As in our usual mode of tabulation, we shall hold constant the individual level attribute.

Table 6.20—Religious Diversity Per Cent Dropping Out

NUMBER OF POSITIONS REPRESENTED IN THE GROUP	INDIVIDUAL RELIGIOUS PREFERENCE							
	Protestant		Catholic		Jewish		None	
1	45	(190)	-	(0)	59	(17)	-	(0)
2	28	(270)	44	(25)	53	(30)	43	(54)
3	35	(280)	34	(65)	30	(82)	24	(67)
4	37	(239)	38	(66)	39	(107)	35	(82)

Here is some support for the diversity hypothesis. We note that for the only two religions with completely homogeneous groups (Protestants and Jews) drop-out is higher in the unanimous situation than in any of the mixed situations. However, we also notice that the effect is not consistent enough to justify the simple proposition that retention increases with diversity. For one thing, there is a slight but consistent tendency for higher drop-outs in the fourth row (Protestant-

Catholic-Jewish-None) than in the third. We also note that among Protestants, the best retention rates are in row two, while among the other religions, the third row does best. The differences are not terribly strong, but they do seem to suggest that Protestants react most favorably to a little heterogeneity, while the other religions react more favorably to moderate heterogeneity, and extreme diversity doesn't help any of the four.

The question now arises whether certain qualitative combinations enter into the picture, in addition to the purely quantitative variable represented by the number of positions to be found in the group. We can look at this by ranking the combinations in terms of drop-out rates, separately for the four positions.

Table 6.21—Religious Composition Per Cent Dropping Out

Group Type	Protestants		Group Type	Catholics		Group Type	Jews		Group Type	None	
P	45%	(190)	PC	43%	(23)	JN	69%	(16)	JN	55%	(11)
P JN	40	(77)	PCJ	43	(28)	J	59	(17)	P N	39	(41)
PCJN	37	(239)	PCJN	38	(66)	PCJ	43	(23)	PCJN	35	(82)
P J	34	(47)	PC N	27	(37)	PCJN	39	(107)	P JN	31	(26)
PC N	34	(143)	C N	-	(2)	P J	36	(14)	PC N	20	(41)
PCJ	32	(60)				P JN	25	(59)			
P N	30	(138)									
PC	20	(85)									

In Table 6.21 the group types are summarized by use of capital letters (e.g., *PCN* means groups consisting of Protestants, Catholics, and Nones), and the types are arranged in order of descending drop-out rates. We can draw a number of conclusions from the table.

First, in terms of our diversity hypothesis, we note that among Protestants, the all Protestant groups have higher drop-out rates than any other type; however, among the Jews, although the *J* type has the second highest drop-out rate, the *JN* type is slightly higher. Since both are based on a handful of cases, it is hard to reach a firm conclusion. We also note that in each of the four groups there is no simple relationship between drop-out and number of positions represented, the most heterogeneous type (*PGJN*) being in the middle in each of the four sub-tables.

What about specific qualitative combinations? We can begin with the Catholics. Since all the Catholic combinations include Protestants, we have no evidence on the effect of Protestants on Catholics. However, when we look at Jews and Nones, there is a hint that the presence of "Nones" has a beneficial effect on Catholic drop-out. We can see this possible trend, by re-casting the data in a fourfold table.

Table 6.22—Jews, Nones, and Per Cent of Catholics Dropping Out

NONES	JEWS			
	Present		Absent	
Present	38%	(66)	27%	(37)
Absent	43	(28)	43	(23)

Table 6.22 shows a slight increase in Catholic retention in groups where Nones are included, regardless of the presence or absence of Jews, although the difference is small. The presence of Jews, controlling for Nones, shows no consistent effect. We should stress that the number of cases is so small that the results are only suggestive.

We can now apply the same analysis to the Jews and Nones, again considering only groups with one or more Protestants.

Table 6.23—Catholics, Nones, and Per Cent of Jews Dropping Out

NONES	CATHOLICS			
	Present		Absent	
Present	39%	(107)	25%	(59)
Absent	43	(23)	36	(14)

Table 6.24—Jews, Catholics, and Per Cent of Nones Dropping Out

CATHOLICS	JEWS			
	Present		Absent	
Present	35%	(82)	20%	(41)
Absent	31	(26)	39	(41)

Table 6.23 shows a slight tendency among the Jews for higher retention when there are Nones in the group, and lower when there are Catholics. However, we remember that the very worst Jewish retention rates are in the *JN* groups, and hence this must be taken with a grain of salt. Table 6.24 shows no consistent trends in terms of effects of Jews and Catholics on drop-out among Nones.

Over-all, we find little evidence that combinations of specific religious positions affect program retention, in terms of comparison among Catholics, Jews, and Nones.

What evidence there is hints that the presence of Nones in a group might have a favorable effect on retention for Catholics, but the effect is so small, in comparison with other compositional variables, that we need not consider it seriously.

A similar analysis, examining the effect of the presence or absence of minority (Catholic-Jewish-None) spokesmen on the retention of Protestants can be performed by re-arranging the materials in the left-hand column of Table 6.21. The arrangement is left as a homework assignment for the reader, but the result is that there is no consistent effect of minority spokesmen on the drop-out of Protestants (although our entire story has not been told).

To sum up: it looks as if the presence of one or more members of a different faith is a favorable sign in terms of retention, although retention is not a straight line function of the number of viewpoints in the group. In terms of specific combinations, we find that the presence or absence of Catholics, Jews, and Nones, has no effect on their retention or on the retention of Protestants.

One logical possibility has been left out, however. What about the effect of Protestants on other religions? Since 93 per cent of the groups have one or more Protestants, our simple presence-absence index is of limited value here, and we will consider this problem in terms of our standard graph, dividing members into Protestants and Non-Protestants, and classifying groups in terms of their proportion of Protestants.

Chart 6.5
Religion and Drop-Out

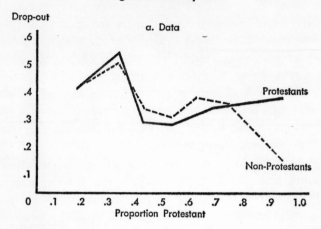

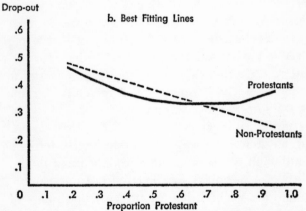

Here is a rather different story. Both Protestants and Non-Protestants seem to show a compositional effect. The effects are not the same though. For Non-Protestants, drop-out decreases as the proportion of Protestants increases. That is, the presence of Protestants tends to increase the retention of Non-Protestants. This is in accord with the diversity hypothesis, for among Non-Protestants, the greater number of

Protestants can be thought of as an increase in the number of people who have a different religious position. If the hypothesis were correct, however, drop-out rates for Protestants should increase with the number of Protestants. Not so, although what they do is a little mysterious. The best fitting line we can get is a parabola, which suggests higher Protestant drop-outs at the two extremes. However, our statistical tests tell us that although the parabola gives a good fit it does not account for much of the variation in drop-out scores among the Protestants. In simpler terms, our statistical tests tell us that a straight line will not fit the Protestant data and a curve will fit, but the curve doesn't do a good job of describing what happens.

One attack on this problem would be to imagine what would happen if two propositions were true: (1) Unanimous agreement with one's religious position is bad for retention and (2) The presence of Protestants is good for retention. Now, if so, what would we expect to find? Among Non-Protestants, we would find that drop-out decreased with P, for as P increases there are more Protestants (Proposition 2) and less chance that the group will agree with one's religious position (Proposition 1). However, among Protestants, we would expect a rise in retention as P moved from zero to .5 (Proposition 2), but after .5 retention should decrease, as more and more of the group tend to agree with a given Protestant member's position. The net effect of these two hypotheses should be two curves rather like those in Chart 6.5 and no wonder, since the hypotheses were deduced to explain it.

When we put all these things together, we have still further support for the diversity hypothesis, although not necessarily for the reasoning which led us to it. If in groups with low proportions of Protestants, we find high drop-out among both groups; in groups fairly evenly divided we find medium drop-out among both groups; and in groups with high proportion of Protestants, low drop-out among Non-Protestants and high drop-out among Protestants, the net effect should be to give

low over-all drop-out rates for groups which are diverse in
their religious composition, i.e. are about half Protestant.
The data support this inference.

Table 6.25—Per Cent Dropping Out, by Religious Composition

PROPORTION PROTESTANT		
0-.39	.40-.59	.60+
45% (322)*	31% (493)*	36% (915)*

* No. of individuals

This then is the case for religious diversity, and we note
that unlike political diversity, it may be of practical significance, since 28 per cent of the members are in the diverse
groups which appear to be benefitting from this process.

Our labors are about to go for nought, though, for in order
to prove our case we should show that religious composition
still relates to program retention, when we control for our
other variables—CAS, status, education, and political composition. This is necessary only, however, if religious composition is related to these variables, and it is.

Table 6.26—Religious Composition and Other Correlates of Retention (per cent of groups which are high on)

	P, PROTESTANT		
	0-.39	.40-.69	.70+
Political Diversity	26%	37%	32%
Educational Diversity	26	11	7
Activity	38	46	46
Contacts	41	43	55
Change in Schools	47	57	49
Status	53	54	72
No. of groups	(34)	(67)	(71)

Regardless of the variable in consideration, the low Protestant group appears disadvantaged. Fewer of them show
political diversity, high activity, outside contacts, or change
in schools, and more of them show educational diversity. The
net result is that by controlling almost any of these, we can

Table 6.27—Religious Composition and Drop-Out, Controlling for Individual Religious Preference and Group Characteristics (per cent dropping out)

P. PROT.	PROTESTANTS			NON-PROTESTANTS		
	0-.39	.40-.69	.70+	0-.39	.49-.69	.70+
P. Democrat						
0-.49	77% (22)	38% (205)	36% (308)	69% (68)	35% (161)	37% (46)
.50-.69	14 (14)	27 (135)	29 (159)	19 (53)	32 (110)	12 (26)
.70+	38 (24)	39 (33)	43 (79)	40 (112)	37 (30)	- (7)
P. Education						
0-.39	64 (11)	25 (63)	64 (58)	49 (37)	20 (54)	- (7)
.40-.49	69 (13)	56 (34)	48 (44)	62 (65)	35 (31)	- (6)
.50+	33 (36)	33 (276)	30 (444)	34 (131)	37 (216)	32 (66)
P. Status						
0-.49	51 (37)	36 (177)	57 (134)	36 (130)	38 (137)	37 (19)
.50+	39 (23)	33 (196)	28 (412)	53 (103)	30 (164)	27 (60)
CAS						
(+++) (++--)	- (8)	32 (99)	21 (193)	5 (39)	25 (87)	19 (16)
(+-+) (--++)	50 (12)	28 (79)	29 (70)	44 (59)	25 (57)	20 (15)
(-+-) (---+)	45 (11)	41 (90)	33 (127)	44 (43)	41 (71)	21 (24)
(---) (+---)	59 (29)	34 (105)	56 (156)	60 (92)	43 (86)	50 (24)

make our religious trends disappear. We shall not go through the entire analysis, but present the summary tables.

Table 6.27 combines four separate tables. We will begin with political composition. Our original analysis suggested that groups with between 50 per cent and 70 per cent Democrats have very good retention experience. Reading across in Table 6.27 we find that in each religious situation, the conclusion still holds. Hence, religion does not wash out political composition. However, among the Protestants, we no longer find a drop-out difference between the lows and mediums and between the mediums and highs. Among the Non-Protestants we have too few cases in one of the crucial cells, but in politically diverse groups, at least, Non-Protestant retention no longer increases with the proportion of Protestants.

Turning now to education, we remember that we have seen high drop-out in the .40-.49 range. In four out of five comparisons the .40-.49 drop-out is higher than the 0-.39, and in four out of five also it is higher in the .40-.49 groups than in the .50 or greater. Thus, religion does not wash out education. However, among the Protestants we find that the low-middle difference holds in only two out of three, and the middle-high in only one out of three. Among the Non-Protestants, the compositional effect washes out in the high education groups, although it may be present in the other two education levels.

Next is status. In five out of six comparisons the predicted retention advantage holds, but the predicted religious effect only appears among Protestants in low status groups and Non-Protestants in high status groups.

Finally, we turn to CAS. We notice that with only a few exceptions our familiar CAS trend appears in each column, but the predicted religious differences only turn up in about half of the comparisons.

In short, although none of these variables completely eliminates the religious effects, in none of them does religious composition maintain a consistent pattern of the type predicted from our analysis.

To summarize: we have probably given the greatest detailed attention to a variable which turns out to be unimportant when we control for other variables known to be important. Over-all, religious composition either in terms of presence or absence of specific religious positions, or in terms of proportion Protestant does not seem to be an independent contributor to program retention.

Two qualifications must be made to this conclusion, however.

First, we feel justified in still maintaining that totally Protestant groups are a fairly bad risk. We have already seen that they have high drop-out rates as compared with other possible combinations of positions. Furthermore, the preceding analysis suggests that they tend to be of high status and high education, both of which are favorable signs; hence, their high drop-out rates can not be explained by deleterious positions on other indexes. We can thus save one shred of our diversity hypothesis by suggesting that perfectly homogeneous groups are not to be encouraged, but among not perfectly homogeneous groups, the nature of the blend of religious positions is not an independent factor in the group level retention process.

Second, it still remains that groups with low proportions of Protestants have high drop-out rates. All other things remaining equal (the most dangerous phrase in the academic world), an increase in the number of low Protestant groups would raise drop-outs in the program, a decrease would raise retention. The point of our analysis is that this would not be *because* of the religious composition, but rather because these groups would also tend to be low on political diversity, activity, outside contacts, and status, and high on educational diversity. These factors, presumably, would account for their contribution to drop-out.

In concluding the analysis of ideological memberships as a group level factor in program retention, we can pull things together by putting our two new characteristics into their appropriate parts of the model. Political preference will appear twice: slight Democratic majorities being both an independent contributor to retention, and also an intervening variable in the relationship between outside contacts and activity. Religious composition will have to be placed out in left field, affecting drop-out only through its correlation with other variables.

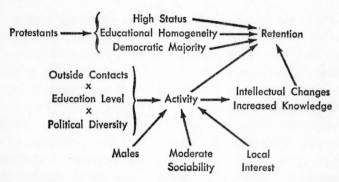

One reason for the lack of coherent patterns on denominational differences may be that although religious ideologies are important, we have been looking at them from the wrong point of view. We do not have a compositional analysis on the following data, but in terms of standard cross-tabulational analysis, we have some evidence that it is not denominational adherence, but rather openness to other religious positions that plays a role in program retention. We will use here a set of items which attempted to tap intellectual acceptance or rejection of a series of religious positions.

Specific religious leanings were measured by asking each respondent to review a list of twelve religious positions (Agnosticism, Atheism, Buddhism, Christian Science, "Fundamentalist" Protestantism, "Liberal" Protestantism, "Middle of the Road" Protestantism, Mohammedanism, Mysticism,

Orthodox Judaism, Reform Judaism, and Thomism or Roman Catholicism). Respondents were asked to check the three systems which they found "most congenial intellectually" and the three they found "least congenial intellectually."

After thrashing about for some time in our analysis, we began to notice a theme. It appeared that endorsement of a given religious position went with higher drop-out rates when the endorser came from a social group for which that position was "natural." The proposition doesn't hold for Catholics or for Thomism as a religious position, but otherwise the pattern is fairly consistent. Table 6.28 summarizes the findings.

The first conclusion we can draw from Table 6.28 is that there is no specific religious ideology which has a uniform effect on drop-out. That is, there is no column with all plus signs or all minus signs.

The second conclusion is that to some degree the data support our idea that drop-out is higher among people who endorse their "appropriate" religious position. Consider the lower status Protestants. If they endorse Fundamentalist Protestantism, their drop-out rates go up, but endorsement of other positions is either favorable or has no effect. High status Protestants, in contrast, are unaffected by endorsement of Fundamentalist Protestantism, but show slightly higher drop-out if they endorse Liberal Protestantism or Reform Judaism, two positions which are more typical of their social milieu. Low status Jews, for whom Orthodox Judaism is the "natural position" show higher drop-out rates when they endorse it, and lower drop-out rates when they endorse Liberal Protestantism or Reform Judaism. High status Jews and Catholics don't fit the pattern, a finding for which undoubtedly we could come up with a clever rationalization if we went to work on it.

One is hardly overwhelmed by the size or consistency of these effects, but the hint is that what is at issue is not en-

Table 6.28—Effect of Religious Ideologies on Drop-Out for Different Religious and Class Groups

Per cent dropping out among those checking "most congenial" minus per cent dropping out among those checking "least congenial" or not checking

RELIGIOUS PREFERENCE AND STATUS	Fundamentalist Protestant	Liberal Protestant	POSITION Orthodox Jewish	Reform Jewish	Thomism
Protestant					
Low	+19 (62, 335)*	−9 (313, 84)	+1 (16, 381)	−1 (105, 292)	+3 (52, 345)
High	0 (67, 382)	+6 (350, 99)	+2 (23, 426)	+10 (131, 318)	+14 (38, 411)
Jewish					
Low	- (0, 86)	−12 (30, 56)	+6 (25, 61)	−27 (70, 16)	- (4, 82)
High	- (3, 120)	+1 (65, 58)	−6 (24, 99)	+3 (100, 23)	- (2, 121)
Catholic					
Low	- (8, 52)	- (9, 51)	0 (21, 39)	+20 (13, 47)	- (55, 5)
High	- (6, 70)	- (14, 62)	+3 (32, 44)	+27 (10, 66)	- (71, 5)

* The first number within each set of parentheses is the case base for those who checked "most congenial"; the second is for those who checked "least congenial" or who did not check the item.

dorsement or rejection of a specific religious ideology, but rather the ability to accept positions which are somewhat new or challenging in terms of previous influences.

We can go about this question somewhat more directly by constructing a new index of religious ideology, based on the combination of answers to these items.

Because each respondent was asked to pick three positions which he found most congenial, it was possible to classify them on the basis of the pattern of combinations, including those who endorsed only one or two religious systems. Our classification is based on a more detailed typology developed by Lathrop Vickery Beale and we are indebted to her for her help in this part of the analysis. We divided the members into three categories. First, there were those whose combinations included only selections from *within* one conventional religious tradition, i.e., Protestantism, Judaism, or Catholicism. Second, there were those combinations that included multiple traditions but only conventional religious systems. Third, were combinations that included at least one of the unconventional systems, i.e., Agnosticism, Atheism, Mysticism, Mohammedanism and Buddhism.

In making these distinctions we are concerned with distinguishing members who are of varying degrees of "open-mindedness" when it comes to religious beliefs and thought systems. The first category, those restricting selections to one conventional religious tradition represent, according to this interpretation, the "closed-minded" individuals. Members who select either multiple conventional traditions or unconventional religious systems can be considered as "open-minded." The closed-minded member would, according to our hypothesis, be somewhat less tolerant of free inquiry into the area of fundamental religious beliefs, and hence, more likely to be offended by the readings and discussions that raise problems in this area. Such a member would be expected to drop out more frequently than the open-minded individual for whom the subject is considerably less sacrosanct.

The following two tables show that controlling for our important individual level correlates there are slight, but consistent (or perhaps consistent, but slight) differences in the drop-out rates of the open and closed minded.

Table 6.29—Religious Open-Mindedness, Age, Education, and Per Cent Dropping Out

AGE & EDUCATION	RELIGIOUS OPEN-MINDEDNESS			
	Closed-Minded		Open-Minded	
Under 35				
Less than AB	43%	(30)	40%	(140)
AB or more	38	(44)	34	(345)
35 and older				
Less than AB	39	(79)	30	(342)
AB or more	33	(86)	24	(482)

Table 6.30—Religious Open-Mindedness, Exposure, Activity, and Per Cent Dropping Out

YEARS OF GREAT BOOKS COMPLETED	ACTIVITY	RELIGIOUS OPEN-MINDEDNESS			
		Closed-Minded		Open-Minded	
0	Active	40%	(20)	26%	(124)
	Inactive	52	(94)	50	(347)
1 or more	Active	22	(45)	16	(381)
	Inactive	32	(71)	28	(407)

Compared with the other variables, the effects of open-mindedness are slight, but since denomination *per se* has no consistent effects, these tables suggest that willingness to consider a range of religious positions may be more important than the denomination which provides the respondent's major religious ideology.

§ Summary

Because these groups meet to engage in serious discussions of religious and political ideas, it can hardly be that the abilities and the ideological positions of the members are irrelevant for the success of the groups. Nevertheless, it is difficult to find generalizations which can pull together all of the disparate findings in this chapter. In the case of social structural variables, although we had to force the fit a little here and there, we think we found a rather consistent pattern in which active participation in the discussion and its consequences affected drop-out, and other roles and social relationships tended to affect retention through influences on the social system of the discussions. Our analysis in this chapter has helped expand this theme, for the findings on education and on political composition suggest that cultural climates influence the CAS process. Generally speaking, climates of political diversity increase role volume and climates of intellectualism make outside contacts a benign rather than malignant variable.

It is in terms of the direct contribution of the cultural variables that problems of interpretation arise. What can we say?

First, it is clear that ideological positions do not affect retention directly. That is, we found no political or religious position whose adherents were more or less likely to stay in the program. We have no evidence that Democrats, Non-Democrats, Protestants, Catholics, Jews, or Atheists vary in retention.

Second, while intellectual ability is certainly necessary for participation, it would appear that such a high proportion of the members fall in the optimal range of abilities that within the program as it is now, differences in intellectual skills are not important in retention.

Third, while it had been our original hypothesis that sheer diversity in ideologies would improve retention by making for a vigorous interchange of ideas in the discussion, we did not find much evidence for this idea. If such were the case we would have found a set of nice dish-shaped curves in which drop-out was higher at extreme P levels for political and religious positions. Nevertheless, the general sweep of the evidence comes closer to this than to any other broad dictum. It would appear that mixtures of political preference are helpful, that all-Protestant groups do not do too well, and perhaps that openness to religious ideas improves retention. No one of these is a clear-cut pattern, and it may be that what is important is willingness to hear a range of ideas rather than availability of a range of spokesmen, because, after all, the books themselves do provide a variety of ideological stimuli. However, taken together, these three findings do build a slight case for the diversity hypothesis.

Does all of this mean that ideas are unimportant for the success of Great Books groups? We would not go that far by any means, if only because the books themselves (which are a constant in our study) provide a wide spectrum of ideas. It might well be that a curriculum which stressed only one ideological position would lead to zooming drop-out rates, and when, in a sense, Plato, Thomas Aquinas, and Karl Marx are present in every group, the presence or absence of live spokesmen doesn't make much difference. What we would say, however, is that in terms of the participants it appears that it is the vigorous discussion of ideas, rather than the convictions or range of convictions of the participants which is the most important aspect of program retention.

7. Summary and Conclusion

*T*he chapters of this report have been concerned, in one way or another, with the factors which keep people in the Great Books program from one year to another, or, more exactly, from 1957 to 1958. The data come from a national sample of almost two thousand Great Books participants who filled out questionnaires in the fall of 1957. One year later NORC managed to establish the continuation status of over 90 per cent of the sample, and the analysis was centered on the differences between members who continued in Great Books and those who dropped out.

Our original sample consisted of the members of 172 discussion groups selected by a probability procedure from United States counties included in NORC's national area probability sample. Just as in those trick pictures which sometimes look like two black profiles against a white background and sometimes like a white vase against a black background, our data can be viewed either as 1909 people who happen to belong to 172 discussion groups, or, alternatively, as 172 discussion groups whose members happen to be the 1909 people in our study. This book amounts to a systematic development of this theme.

Chapter 1 treated problem and method. Both are somewhat off the beaten track. The research problem is that of the maintenance of a social system, the factors which explain why some groups flourish and others peter out. By appeal to authority and common sense we claimed that while such problems are usually attacked on the broad scale of historical studies, small groups actually are a particularly strategic place to make such studies. The methodological sections of the chapter set forth in detail the logic involved in looking at the same materials not only as group data or individual data, but trying to do both simultaneously. A technique was reported whereby each respondent received two scores on each variable in the study. For instance, each male was coded as a male and also coded in terms of the proportion of members of his group who were males. By looking at men and women separately and looking at each sex in groups which varied in their proportion of men, we could look for the effects of sex as an individual attribute and also effects of the sex composition of the groups. The general point has been well made by many others, and what we added was essentially a classification of some of the possibilities which can turn up. The last part of the chapter outlined a classification of the types of relationships which may be found in this approach, which we call compositional analysis.

Chapter 2 described the kinds of people in our sample, and by contrasting them with scattered data from other sources, suggested some of the ways in which Great Books members are selected, in the sense of being unrepresentative of Americans in general. The variables involved were heavily concentrated among social structural characteristics which are indexes of the roles played in the larger society, both because this is the sociologist's natural way of describing people and also because these are the variables which turned out to be important in subsequent chapters. In general, Great Books members tend to be highly educated, upper middle class, young, married people. They appear highly involved in their communities, and while undoubtedly highly over-intellectual in comparison with the general population are essentially "middle brows" rather than esoteric cult seekers.

Interestingly, they appear less upwardly mobile than comparison groups and come to the program seeking intellectual stimulation in the discussions rather than uplift or self-help.

Chapter 3 switched from people to roles, or rather from roles in the larger social structure to roles in the small discussion groups. Data were presented to document the claim that there is a role system in the discussions characterized by mutual expectations and a division of labor or role differentiation along with considerable overlap. To a large extent, the distribution and frequency of these roles is a function of carry-over from situations outside the group rather than an internal development from the discussion process. In this chapter we outlined some personal characteristics associated with role playing. Hardly unexpectedly, intellectual preparation and background play a major part in determining whether a given member will be named as active in the discussions. Kinship roles are very important also, and sex and marital status are major predictors. Detailed analysis suggested that role propensities developed in families have a strong carry-over into non-family situations such as Great Books, even extending to a difference in the activity levels of married women depending on whether their husbands attend, and, if they attend, whether they are active. Chapters 4, 5, and 6 although devoted to another topic, extended this analysis by suggesting that social climates outside the groups affect role structures in the Great Books discussions.

Chapters 4, 5, and 6 applied the techniques developed in Chapter 1 to the variables described in Chapters 2 and 3 in order to explain variations in membership loss from group to group.

Chapter 4 analysed the effects of formal and informal roles in the groups. Both in terms of individual level differences and group compositional differences activity in a discussion role is strongly associated with retention. Groups with many active members hold more of their members, and within groups of a given proportion active, those who are named as playing a role are more likely to stay. The particular kind of role, in terms of differentiation of function, shows no association with retention. High levels of role activity are associated with high levels of reported favorable effects of participation in Great Books, which also help retention. Generally speaking, high proportions of members who see each other outside the meetings are associated with high rates of activity, but such outside contacts do not contribute independently toward retention. Outside contacts, activity levels, and program effects are associated in such a fashion as to suggest a process (CAS) whereby social interaction outside the groups leads to high volumes of participation in the discussion, which in turn lead to favorable effects of participation. In terms of formally defined roles, leader training and acceptance or rejection of the discussion techniques recommended by The Great Books Foundation have no relationship with drop-out when one controls for variables in the CAS chain, but there is a little evidence that in the cases where the members want the leaders to use a specific discussion technique and the leaders do not, drop-out is higher.

Chapter 5 was devoted to roles outside the program itself. We found that in terms of group composition high proportions of high status members or high proportions who are active in community affairs are associated with high retention. In addition we found that high proportions of males, moderate proportions who are sociable in terms of informal visiting, and high proportions interested in community affairs are favorable signs. These latter three variables, however, do not contribute independently when one controls for the volume of role activity. We concluded that large numbers of men, moderate proportions of social members, and high proportions with local interests are part of the CAS process, and illustrate further the ways in which these groups are affected by their ties to the outside community.

Chapter 6 treated intellectual and ideological variables, both as contributors to program retention and also as factors in the CAS process. High scores on a measure of knowledge of liberal arts appeared to behave similarly to other effect variables in the CAS scheme. Compositionally, education showed a curvilinear relationship, with higher drop-outs in groups characterized by 40 per cent to 49 per cent college graduates. Our measure of reading sophistication, in terms of the brow level of books read outside the program, showed what we call a type IV relationship. Low brow readers are more likely to stay with the program in groups where they are in a minority but non-low brow readers are not affected by the composition. Education was also shown to affect the CAS process. Among highly educated people, outside contacts lead to higher activity levels, but among less educated people high volumes of outside contacts are associated with lower role volume. We interpreted this relationship as indicating that when the values of the outside world are in agreement with the group's purposes close interpersonal relationships outside the program will inhibit active discussion participation. In terms of religion, religious composition showed a complicated set of effects whose meaning was hard to interpret. Generally, though, we concluded that open mindedness of religious matters and some diversity in religious positions is a good sign. In terms of politics, we found no individual level difference, but groups with a slight majority of Democrats had better records than groups which were more homogeneous. Individual level analyses showed little effect of politics or religious denomination *per se*. Individual level analysis of intellectual variables suggested a curvilinear relationship in that members who were low on all of our measures had higher drop-out rates, but the small number who were high on all measures also had slightly higher drop-out experience.

Can we now pull together in three or four crisp generalizations the major conclusions of our study? No, unless we are willing to settle for truisms, for the major conclusion of our study would be that program retention in Great Books is extremely complicated. A complete picture of the factors involves individual characteristics, group characteristics, characteristics which work one way at the group level and another at the individual level, characteristics which work one way in some subclasses and another way in others, characteristics whose meaning is clear but whose effects are obscure, and characteristics whose effects are clear but whose meaning is obscure.

Since, however, elaborate research efforts frequently fail even to document truisms, it may be well to list some of the themes which have developed.

§ Groups Are Important

None of the authors of this report is an expert in the sociological specialty known as small groups. Hence, we are not grinding sub-disciplinary axes when we conclude that throughout the analysis we have been struck by the importance of group discussion and group relationships as factors in program retention. The group not only provides an efficient administrative resource by which a national program can be maintained without an expensive staff of professional instructors; it also appears that in the discussion process and in the social relationships which it develops or reinforces, there is a powerful cement which binds the members together and provides a major gratification from participation. We should make it clear that nothing in this conclusion should be read as suggesting that intellectual and cerebral aspects of Great Books are unimportant. Quite to the contrary, the frequency with which intellectual characteristics turn out to be important for the individual and for the group suggest that it is precisely the combination of challenging intellectual content and group discussion as a medium which explain the vitality of Great Books groups.

§ Preparation Is Important

Although it has never been dignified by presentation as a formal law, the one generalization which almost always turns up in surveys of intellectual matters is—"Them as has gets." That is, books on specific subjects are bought, not by people who know nothing about the subject, but by people who are already informed, programs of mass persuasion tend to reach mostly people who are already persuaded, and programs for uplift tend to reach only those who are already uplifted. Great Books is no exception to this rule, and throughout our analysis we have seen that Great Books tends to keep, not those who have needed the most intellectual growth, but those whose preparation and interest are already strong. This is not all there is to the story, for some evidence in Chapter 6 suggested that the super-intellectuals have high drop-out rates. The true relationship is probably curvilinear, with high losses among the least prepared and among those who have little need for the program. However, the relative sizes of these groups in our society is such that the program hardly need fear that it runs much risk of lowering retention by recruiting well prepared members.

§ Discussion Activity Is Important

By now the typewriter keys which spell "activity" should be worn down to their roots from the frequency with which that word has appeared in this report. It is clear that whether viewed as a personal characteristic or as a group characteristic, large numbers of people who are seen by the other group members as active participants are very favorable for retention. We now know a lot about the effects of activity, and we learned a lot about where it comes from. What we don't know is what it is. Our data are unable to tell us whether this measure taps 1) sheer decibel volume of discussion, 2) evenness of participation versus domination by a few members, or 3) whether it is an index of some subtle inter-personal characteristic such as group cohesion or integration of role structure.

Furthermore, there is a famous example in social science which indicates that off-hand speculation on a finding like this is dangerous. A set of studies by Kurt Lewin conducted during World War II suggested that personal decisions made during group discussions were more binding than those made alone.[1] These findings, which have been replicated a number of times, were quickly seized upon by group dynamic partisans and applied to all sorts of practical situations. However, more recent experiments which have attempted to control the precise aspects of the social process involved suggest that discussion *per se* is not terribly important; rather, the effectiveness of discussion as a technique for influence seems to lie in such things as forcing one to come to some sort of decision and in the perception of group consensus on the issue.[2]

From this point of view, although activity as we have measured it appears to be the keystone in the retention process, we have not achieved a clear-cut theoretical understanding of this variable and the intervening social and psychological processes which make it so important. However, we are tempted to suggest the following interpretation, which makes a certain amount of sense to us. It seems to us that people come to a discussion either to listen or to talk or both. Now, if talking is gratifying, the more opportunities one has to

1. These studies are summarized in Kurt Lewin, "Group Decision and Social Change," in Eleanor E. Maccoby, Theodore M. Newcomb, and Eugene L. Hartley, *Readings in Social Psychology* (New York: 1958, Henry Holt and Company), pp. 197-211.

2. Cf. Edith Bennett Pelz, "Some Factors in Group Decision" in Maccoby, Newcomb, and Hartley, *op. cit.,* pp. 212-219.

talk, the more satisfying the situation would be. Conversely, if listening is gratifying, the more people who are talking the more likely it is that one will hear something interesting. Thus, it may be that the individual level advantage of the actives is related to the increased opportunities for talking, and the compositional effect is related to increased opportunities for listening. Activity from this point of view is not an aspect of the discussion process. It *is* the discussion process.

§ Groups Are Affected by Social Structure

Life apparently does not begin anew when one sits around a table to discuss the Great Books. To a large degree patterns and habits of interaction which are learned in roles and social systems outside the program have a measurable impact on the role structure and continuity of the discussion groups. The point is not amazing when one considers the number of hours that people have invested in learning to be a man or woman or spouse or neighbor compared with the brief period of exposure to the program. What is perhaps a little more interesting is the strength of these effects and the relative failure of intrinsic aspects of the group process, such as role function or leadership, to affect the outcome.

We would be among the first to grant that Great Books groups are hardly representative of group life, but we do feel that if our materials have any suggestion beyond application to this program for adult liberal education, the suggestion is that sociologists have tended to overemphasize the degree of insulation between role systems. One of the major points which sociology makes to freshmen and other non-sociologists is that much behavior is role determined and that the same person behaves rather differently when he plays different roles. Similarities in a given person's performance of different roles have been assumed to reflect idiosyncratic aspects of "personality." Our picture of role behavior is somewhat more complex. It suggests that any given social system is affected not only by its own norms and roles and idiosyncratic personalities, but also by the roles and relationships which should have been checked at the door. To the extent then that individuals play a large number of roles and sets of individuals interact in different role contexts, their behavior in a given social setting can be expected to be a rather complex function of the current situation and its structure along with the carry-over and residues from habits and inter-personal patterns from the outside. From this point of view the analysis of social structure is not completed by a catalogue of roles. It is only completed when a cross-referencing is added which shows how role systems interact to affect behavior.

§ Suggestions

It would be quite satisfying if we could now write out a simple prescription for practical advice on program retention in Great Books. However, as we have noted, the relationships discovered in this study are not such as to lead to easy rules of thumb. However, we do feel that some suggestions can be made on the basis of our findings.

First, it would seem that the status quo, in terms of member characteristics, is essentially favorable for program retention. That is, those variables which seem to characterize the Great Books member also seem generally favorable for program retention. Thus, Great Books members tend to be highly educated, and high education is a favorable sign for groups and individuals; Great Books members tend to be active and interested in their communities, another good omen; Great Books members tend toward political diversity, again a positive factor; Great Books members tend to be of high social status, a favorable characteristic; and so on. In general, Great

Books tends to attract disproportionately the kinds of people who have high potentialities for forming viable groups.

There are, however, three exceptions which should be noted.

First, Great Books has a slight disproportion of females. While sex is not an independent contributor to program retention, we have seen that femininity is associated with lower activity in discussion, and that groups with high proportions of women have greater loss rates.

Second, our first survey suggested that Great Books may tend to attract relatively more younger adults than older adults. The analysis in Chapter 5 suggested that these younger adults are at a stage in the life cycle when other responsibilities and involvements compete with Great Books.

Third, although we have stressed the tentativeness of the conclusions, our data do suggest that the program's official leadership style may have some negative consequences. While the problems of leader training are enormously difficult, it would appear that a training program which would permit leaders greater flexibility of technique and adaptation of techniques to specific group needs might boost retention. (However, we do not suggest that hypothetical increases in retention necessarily outweigh positive effects of this technique, untapped by our survey. The negative consequences are not that strong.)

Even though the status quo is essentially healthy, can we make suggestions for improvements? Returning to the logic of our compositional effects analysis, two formal possibilities arise. First, one can seek to change patterns of recruitment for the program. This amounts to changing the mean "*P*-level" in the population. Second, one could think of rearranging the existing groups in such a way as to develop more effective balances of membership characteristics. On the whole, the case for the first approach is strong, the case for the second is weak. While rearrangement has a certain intellectual elegance, two arguments can be made against it. First, it is fairly impractical, for it would require data on members and groups which are generally unavailable (unless each new member is to be asked to fill out the NORC questionnaire), and second it can be shown mathematically that rearrangement will only add to net program retention when there is a *curvilinear* compositional effect at issue. In our data, the only important curvilinear relationships are education, political composition, and informal visiting. Of these, probably only education is amenable to practical manipulation. The program might well consider taking steps to avoid the existence of groups with about 40 per cent college graduates. Our data suggest that these groups (which are quite infrequent) would do better if the college graduates were shifted to another group.

While the rearrangement possibilities are limited, our data do suggest some situations where careful recruiting might yield fairly durable groups. The program might well consider the following sources of new members.

1) *Corporations and Business Firms.* If Great Books could recruit new groups from executives and managers in specific businesses or firms, a cluster of favorable characteristics would appear. Such groups would tend to be of high status, high education (particularly if one could tap their professional staffs—engineers, lawyers, accountants), have high outside contacts (since the members would know each other on the job), and have a high proportion of males.

2) *Civic Organizations.* Since high levels of community interest and activity, high status, and moderate sociability, along with outside contacts appear to be favorable characteristics, recruitment from members of existing civic organizations, such as bar associations, medical societies, civic improvement groups, businessmen's associations, etc. might well provide groups of high potential. One is tempted to add P.T.A.'s, and The League of Women Voters, except that over-femininity is not a good sign.

3) *Middle Aged Couples.* One way of guaranteeing outside contacts and at least 50 per cent males would be to utilize already established groups of married couples. If, in addition, these couples were in the over-35 age group, another positive characteristic could be added. Thus, the infiltration of existing reading circles, hobby groups, and possibly bridge groups (although one has to look out for the extremely high sociability groups) might be good strategy.

A number of examples could be presented, but the general idea is that existing groups with high proportions of males, and/or high-educated people, and/or community actives, and/or high status should all generate strong Great Books groups.

Another strategy, however, is suggested as a complement to drawing Great Books members from existing sociometric networks. We found in Chapter 6 that there was one type of group for which outside contacts were not a favorable sign. These were low education groups. Although people whose intellectual backgrounds are not strong are fairly dubious prospects from the viewpoint of retention, they apparently do better when there is a low volume of outside contacts. This suggests that for such groups recruitment through the mass media (newspapers, posters, radio, etc.) would be effective in that the members might not have common outside relationships which dampen the effects of Great Books.

In short, our data suggest two complementary strategies for forming new groups. On the one hand, it might be wise to look for *extant* groups of people with strong intellectual backgrounds, and, on the other, try to form *brand new* groups for people with weaker intellectual backgrounds. Such complementary approaches would take advantage of the complex relationships between contacts, activity, and retention which were spelled out in Chapter 4.

APPENDIX

Raw Data for Charts in Chapters Three through Six

Chart 3.2—Religious Preference and Discussion Activity

	PROPORTION PROTESTANT						
	0-.29	.3-.39	.4-.49	.5-.59	.6-.69	.7-.79	.8-1.0
Protestant							
Drop-Out	13	3	16	69	46	55	175
Stay	31	21	47	111	111	104	257
	44	24	63	180	157	159	432
Non-Protestants							
Drop-Out	80	10	26	72	34	19	15
Stay	138	35	52	85	52	34	21
	218	45	78	157	86	53	36

Chart 4.1—Exposure and Drop-Out

	PROPORTION ZERO EXPOSURE				
	0-.19	.2-.29	.3-.39	.4-.59	.6-1.0
Zero Years					
Drop-Out	18	26	12	28	233
Stay	19	27	19	42	222
	37	53	31	70	455
One or two years					
Drop-Out	66	44	14	10	21
Stay	207	76	37	35	30
	273	120	51	45	51
Three or more					
Drop-Out	67	24	7	6	6
Stay	205	53	14	25	14
	272	77	21	31	20

Chart 4.2—Outside Contacts and Drop-Out

PROPORTION WITH ONE OR MORE

	0-.39	.4-.49	.5-.59	.6-.69	.7-.79	.8-.89	.9-1.0
One or more							
Drop-Out	11	31	42	51	48	32	103
Stay	11	55	83	91	97	84	229
	22	86	125	142	145	116	332
None							
Drop-Out	49	58	56	29	24	7	14
Stay	47	82	83	75	55	30	23
	96	140	139	104	79	37	37

Chart 4.3—Discussion Activity and Drop-Out

PROPORTION ACTIVE

	0-.19	.2-.29	.3-.39	.4-.49	.5-.59	.6-.69	.7-1.0
Active							
Drop-Out	16	14	29	30	24	17	21
Stay	31	30	76	78	109	83	81
	47	44	105	108	133	100	102
Inactive							
Drop-Out	242	42	71	56	34	21	7
Stay	213	83	109	80	79	36	18
	455	125	180	136	113	57	25

Chart 4.4—Impact and Drop-Out

PROPORTION REPORTING HIGH IMPACT

	0-.19	.2-.29	.3-.39	.4-.49	.5-.59	.6-.69	.7-1.0
Highs							
Drop-Out	11	20	32	55	44	28	30
Stay	21	33	47	85	135	81	89
	32	53	79	140	179	109	119
Lows							
Drop-Out	77	74	57	79	42	22	11
Stay	130	86	93	94	111	40	22
	207	160	150	173	153	62	33

Chart 4.5—Effect on Problem I and Drop-Out

PROPORTION REPORTING ANY EFFECT

	0-.29	.3-.39	.4-.49	.5-.59	.6-.69	.7-1.0
Any Effect						
Drop-Out	25	29	24	21	12	2
Stay	46	91	84	91	30	46
	71	120	108	112	42	48
No Effect						
Drop-Out	231	106	53	45	12	4
Stay	302	217	132	86	20	18
	533	323	185	131	32	22

Chart 4.6—Change in Acceptability of Schools and Drop-Out

	PROPORTION CHANGING				
	0-.29	.3-.39	.4-.49	.5-.59	.6-.69
Changers					
Drop-Out	25	24	37	12	4
Stay	70	68	71	50	66
	95	92	108	62	70
Non-Changers					
Drop-Out	298	87	50	22	9
Stay	450	167	142	48	34
	748	254	192	70	43

Chart 4.7—Ideal Leader: Squelch and Drop-Out

	PROPORTION SQUELCH					
	0-.39	.4-.49	.5-.59	.6-.69	.7-.79	.8-1.0
Squelch						
Drop-Out	12	31	40	93	64	82
Stay	19	56	100	116	155	162
	31	87	140	209	219	244
Not squelch						
Drop-Out	60	64	39	61	40	24
Stay	58	88	113	95	76	46
	118	152	152	156	116	70

Chart 4.8—Ideal Leader: Summarize and Drop-Out

	PROPORTION SUMMARIZE					
	0-.29	.3-.39	.4-.49	.5-.59	.6-.69	.7-1.0
Summarize						
Drop-Out	21	34	43	83	24	46
Stay	40	43	69	93	26	30
	61	77	112	176	50	76
Not Summarize						
Drop-Out	102	81	56	83	19	16
Stay	303	141	159	129	23	17
	405	222	215	212	42	33

Chart 4.9—Ideal Leader: Background and Drop-Out

	PROPORTION BACKGROUND					
	0-.19	.2-.29	.3-.39	.4-.49	.5-.59	.6-1.0
Background						
Drop-Out	10	28	38	36	14	24
Stay	13	33	49	51	22	30
	23	61	87	87	36	54
Not Background						
Drop-Out	140	114	100	71	19	12
Stay	316	250	151	102	26	22
	456	364	251	173	45	34

Chart 4.10—Ideal Leader: Refrain and Drop-Out

	PROPORTION REFRAIN					
	0-.39	.4-.49	.5-.59	.6-.69	.7-.79	.8-1.0
Refrain						
Drop-Out	16	14	42	105	62	101
Stay	5	23	131	136	135	225
	21	37	173	241	197	326
Not Refrain						
Drop-Out	36	21	59	80	34	31
Stay	41	36	131	98	73	44
	77	57	190	178	107	75

Chart 4.11—Ideal Leader: Cross-examine and Drop-Out

	PROPORTION CROSS-EXAMINE						
	0-.29	.3-.39	.4-.49	.5-.59	.6-.69	.7-.79	.8-1.0
C.R.							
Drop-Out	10	35	38	56	50	48	19
Stay	18	41	85	128	77	69	44
	28	76	123	184	127	117	63
Not C.R.							
Drop-Out	62	87	97	66	34	23	8
Stay	118	116	133	154	60	37	12
	170	203	230	220	94	60	20

Chart 5.1—Marital Status and Drop-Out

	PROPORTION MARRIED						
	0-.39	.4-.49	.5-.59	.6-.69	.7-.79	.8-.89	.9-1.0
Married							
Drop-Out	9	19	15	47	62	82	190
Stay	20	30	35	71	107	194	401
	29	49	50	118	169	276	591
Single							
Drop-Out	38	25	22	27	17	22	12
Stay	47	37	21	34	35	34	13
	85	62	43	61	52	56	25

Chart 5.2—Age and Drop-Out

	PROPORTION YOUNG							
	0-.19	.2-.29	.3-.39	.4-.49	.5-.59	.6-.69	.7-.79	.8-1.0
Young								
Drop-Out	13	8	13	48	67	38	63	93
Stay	10	17	28	47	135	68	95	144
	23	25	41	95	202	106	158	237
Older								
Drop-Out	75	10	27	53	45	13	19	12
Stay	147	64	49	69	117	49	30	19
	222	74	76	122	162	62	49	31

Chart 5.3—Sex and Drop-Out

	PROPORTION MALE					
	0-.29	.3-.39	.4-.49	.5-.59	.6-.69	.7-1.0
Male						
Drop-Out	42	50	47	34	25	13
Stay	62	69	121	90	47	41
	104	119	168	124	72	54
Female						
Drop-Out	185	84	77	38	15	4
Stay	265	140	148	69	29	15
	450	224	225	107	44	19

Chart 5.4—Socio-Economic Status and Drop-Out

	PROPORTION HIGH STATUS						
	0-.29	.3-.39	.4-.49	.5-.59	.6-.69	.7-.79	.8-1.0
High Status							
Drop-Out	15	24	37	44	55	41	44
Stay	16	42	65	108	138	99	96
	31	66	102	152	193	140	140
Low Status							
Drop-Out	73	50	59	47	38	15	4
Stay	87	79	78	85	65	35	12
	160	129	137	132	103	50	16

Chart 5.5—Local Interest and Drop-Out

	PROPORTION LOCAL						
	0-.19	.2-.29	.3-.39	.4-.49	.5-.59	.6-.69	.7-1.0
Local							
Drop-Out	9	27	19	33	32	33	26
Stay	13	30	41	48	67	81	65
	22	57	60	81	99	114	91
Non-local							
Drop-Out	93	64	37	46	26	17	5
Stay	104	90	89	65	63	43	21
	197	154	126	111	89	60	26

Chart 5.6—Joiners and Drop-Out

	PROPORTION JOINER					
	0-.29	.3-.39	.4-.49	.5-.59	.6-.69	.7-1.0
Joiners						
Drop-Out	28	28	35	63	46	62
Stay	37	38	66	167	107	141
	65	66	101	230	153	203
Non-Joiners						
Drop-Out	120	53	51	63	29	21
Stay	138	75	88	135	59	28
	258	128	139	198	88	49

Chart 5.7—Sociability and Drop-Out

PROPORTION SOCIABLE

	0-.29	.3-.39	.4-.49	.5-.59	.6-.69	.7-.79	.8-1.0
Sociable							
Drop-Out	19	25	29	45	92	19	56
Stay	32	67	78	107	132	33	62
	51	92	107	152	224	52	118
Less-Sociable							
Drop-Out	78	59	36	46	45	9	11
Stay	122	117	101	88	78	9	11
	200	176	137	134	123	18	22

Chart 6.1—Knowledge Score and Drop-Out

PROPORTION HIGH

	0-.29	.3-.39	.4-.49	.5-.59	.6-.69	.7-.79	.8-1.0
High							
Drop-Out	20	31	38	35	85	26	32
Stay	32	46	76	104	166	65	102
	52	77	114	139	251	91	134
Low							
Drop-Out	107	77	61	36	59	10	7
Stay	134	76	99	88	81	22	14
	241	153	160	124	140	32	21

Chart 6.2—Level of Most Worthwhile Book and Drop-Out

PROPORTION MIDDLEBROW

	0-.29	.3-.39	.4-.49	.5-.59	.6-.69	.7-1.0
Middle Brow						
Drop-Out	24	23	21	40	26	37
Stay	50	45	41	63	33	34
	74	68	62	103	59	71
High Brow						
Drop-Out	106	38	20	30	9	6
Stay	266	101	66	64	27	12
	372	139	86	94	36	18

Chart 6.3—Education and Drop-Out

PROPORTION COLLEGE GRADUATES

	0-.29	.3-.39	.4-.49	.5-.59	.6-.69	.7-.79	.8-1.0
AB+							
Drop-Out	8	16	44	61	61	54	85
Stay	19	28	47	136	132	101	213
	27	44	91	197	193	155	298
<AB							
Drop-Out	41	32	64	60	46	17	11
Stay	50	50	51	99	68	36	31
	91	82	115	159	114	53	42

Chart 6.4—Political Preference and Drop-Out

PROPORTION DEMOCRATS

	0-.29	.3-.39	.4-.49	.5-.59	.6-.69	.7-.79	.8-1.0
Democratic							
Drop-Out	16	47	40	32	48	26	62
Stay	36	56	74	105	104	68	70
	52	103	114	137	152	94	132
Non-Democratic							
Drop-Out	77	80	75	25	29	16	11
Stay	158	111	74	99	67	28	11
	235	191	149	124	96	44	22

Chart 6.5—Religion and Drop-Out

PROPORTION PROTESTANT

	0-.29	.3-.39	.4-.49	.5-.59	.6-.79	.8-1.0
Protestant						
Drop-Out	16	12	17	50	99	152
Stay	22	10	41	120	195	245
	38	22	58	170	294	397
Non-Protestant						
Drop-Out	80	22	26	45	49	5
Stay	111	20	48	102	81	24
	191	42	74	147	130	29

INDEX

Index